Showcasing new

approaches to

higher education

Innovations in Learning and Teaching

Edited by

Christine Penman and Monika Foster

-m-
MERCHISTON PUBLISHING
www.merchistonpublishing.com

First published in 2016 by Merchiston Publishing
Colinton Road, Edinburgh, EH10 5DT
**Staffed by students on the MSc Publishing programme
at Edinburgh Napier University:**
Rachel Aitken, Laura Borrelli, Justine Bottles, Julia Crawford,
Michelle Dalton, Adam Harris, Kirsty Hunter, Nathaniel Kunitskaya,
Lisa Harwood MacKenzie, Jason O'Neill, Romi Rellum

**Generously supported by
The Edinburgh Napier University Teaching Development Fund,
The Edward Clark Trust**

ISBN: 978-0-9576882-8-5

Printed by Bell & Bain Ltd, Glasgow, G46 7UQ
Typeset in Adobe Garamond Pro 11/13

Contents

1 Importing new philosophies into course design

2 Developing a student-centred programme of study

Acknowledgements

We gratefully acknowledge the funding received from the Edinburgh Napier University Teaching Development Fund and the Edward Clark Trust for the publishing of this book.

We would also like to thank the reviewers who set aside precious time for the double-blind peer review process.

Last but not least, we would like to recognise the instrumental role played by Avril Gray, David McCluskey, and their MSc Publishing students: Rachel Aitken, Laura Borrelli, Justine Bottles, Julia Crawford, Michelle Dalton, Adam Harris, Nathaniel Kunitskaya, Lisa Harwood MacKenzie, Kirsty Hunter, Jason O'Neill, and Romi Rellum, who embraced this publishing project with enthusiasm and professionalism from the very start.

Editorial Note

Christine Penman and Monika Foster

"The learning landscape is a restless space."
— Locker (2009), p.139 —

In the literature on teaching and learning in higher education, references to novelty and innovation are regularly tied with the implicit recognition that evolving contexts and modalities of learning preclude static views of pedagogy. This edited collection of chapters subscribes to this dynamic approach by giving voice to academics from different disciplines who have all embarked on a quest to question, challenge and rethink existing practices with a view to test alternative methods, the recombination of parameters, or the re-organisation of learning environments and curriculum design. How can we…? is often the starting point of a journey through the research literature and the trying and testing of alternative ways of doing. With a focus on student experience, innovation, and internationalisation, this edited collection holistically partakes in the Strategy 2020 of Edinburgh Napier University, the institution which has fostered these reflections.

The four different sections of the book articulate the import of new philosophies into course design, the development of student-centred programmes of study, the use of technology and innovative practices in the classroom, and the development of a global outlook through pedagogical activities. Drawing from specific academic disciplines, they widen the frame for reflection by seeking to engage the reader with a range of key questions, which can in turn enrich their own practice: what are the benefits and risks of embedding entrepreneurship and/or professional practice into a course or programme (Richard Whitecross, Isla Kapasi, Avril Gray)? How can we find new ways of engaging students with arduous concepts (Jennifer Murray)? How best to compose an integrated and supportive programme of study (Julia Fotheringham and Kathryn James, Keith Walker and Stephen Robertson)? What are the best ways to foster effective group dynamics (Kirsten MacLeod)? How can we harness technology to support learning (Stephen Robertson and

Sarah Sholl, Laurence Patterson, Mabel Victoria)? How can a programme of study contribute to the widening of perspectives (Rachel Younger, Myrna MacLeod and Ian Macdonald)?

The student-centeredness of this collective endeavour came full circle by being entrusted to a team of students on an MSc Publishing programme who were responsible for the design and the launch of the book into the wider world to generate further conversations. We, as editors, have benefited from the close work with colleagues and students on this publication, which challenges our own thinking and expands our horizons, and are very pleased to offer this edited collection in the hope that it will inspire minds and spark innovative ideas in teaching and learning.

Christine Penman
Senior Lecturer, Languages Subject Group Leader, Edinburgh Napier University
Co-editor Christine Penman has dedicated much of her career to language and multi-modal communication teaching and research. Her theoretical and applied interests are in cultural and cross-cultural aspects of consumption with a particular focus on advertising. As a Fellow of the Higher Education Academy, her research on pedagogical initiatives places an emphasis on the internationalisation of the curriculum. Her research outputs span these two areas of research interests in the form of national and international publications and conference presentations.

Dr Monika Foster
Associate Professor, Business School Academic Lead: Learning and Teaching, Edinburgh Napier University
Dr Monika Foster is a Principal Fellow of the Higher Education Academy with substantial experience in pedagogical design and research outputs, placing her well in her position as co-editor of *Innovations in Learning and Teaching*. Monika's research interests lie in the linguistic, academic and cultural challenges faced by international students in cross-border education. Her recent research includes a scoping study of international student transitions as part of the QAA Enhancement Theme Transitions, a cross-university qualitative research study on exploring staff perceptions of internationalisation of the curriculum and a Santander-funded research project on the motivations of South American students to study in the UK. She has published edited collections and pedagogic books nationally and internationally.

References

Locker, P. (2009) Conclusions – The Learning Landscape: views with endless possibilities. In: Bell, L., Stevenson, H., and Neary, M. (Eds.). *The Future of Higher Education: Policy, Pedagogy and the Student Experience*. London: Continuum International Publishing Group, 139–147.

Foreword

Brian Webster-Henderson

The annual conference run by the Teaching Fellows Community at Edinburgh Napier University provides an occasion for the academic community to share good practice and pedagogical research or evaluation; it also provides an opportunity for networking, the importance of which can never be underestimated. This year the conference ignited new ideas and the concept for this book was developed. This book (and eBook) provides a further opportunity for the dissemination of innovation and good practice from the University community.

The book is organised into four key sections: *Importing new philosophies into course design*; *Developing a student-centred programme of study*; *Digital technology and innovative practices in the classroom*; and *Developing a global outlook through pedagogical activities*. Each provides insights into the current or emerging priorities for this University, though of course the institution as a whole excels in many other areas.

Within my own discipline of nursing and healthcare, and as my academic career matures, I am constantly reminded of the power of innovation within the area of higher education. Some years ago, I guest-edited an edition of a key nursing journal called *Nurse Education Today* (Clark and Webster, 2012). As part of that editorial, my colleague and I identified the necessary attributes for innovation to flourish in academic life:

> Successful innovation in the design and delivery of education requires a genuine passion for education, a shared commitment to excellence and student centredness, and a positive environment that fosters creativity and harnesses the talents and imagination of staff (ibid, p.729).

Equally, we identified that whilst everyone can engage in innovative practice, having the right conditions within a higher education institution is of paramount importance.

As an academic, I am fascinated by the role that these institutions have to play in the science of learning and knowledge. I am often drawn to the work of Ron Barnett, an academic I have held in high esteem for many years. Barnett's breadth of work is fascinating; his insights into higher education academically stretching, challenging, and rewarding all at the same time. In his work *Realising the University in an Age of Super Complexity* (2000), Barnett identifies the complex roles that universities play in relation to learning, society, citizenship, and constructs of power. He espouses the theory that higher education institutions are not only complex organisations for students and staff, but often *supercomplex* organisations; and yet, they must still be required to provide a meaningful, important, and socially empowering education. I would suggest that we currently find ourselves in complex times as a higher education section. As policymakers and academics discuss and occasionally argue over teaching excellence and its many possible definitions, the role of quality metrics in aiding customer choice, the challenges of widening access, and future funding for the higher education sector, it can be easy to forget that students are at the heart of these discussions. Whether or not we agree with Barnett regarding his theory of the supercomplexity of higher education, students are the key driver to all that we do. Whether we can easily define teaching excellence or not, students are the best critics of our education; in relation to our innovative pedagogical practice, it is our students who benefit, develop, and will hopefully remember the value of that innovation.

This book identifies a range of innovations within a complex, supercomplex, and ever-changing higher education environment. They reflect a journey of realisation and development by the authors and by the institution as a whole. They come from a range of disciplines and academic staff at varying stages of their career journeys and so reflect a richness of insight, change, scale, and creativity. In publishing this book, it is the desire of the editors that it will be a narrative of dissemination which will also provide an opportunity for critical discourse across the academic and student community: a narrative that reflects innovation within a world of complexity and supercomplexity.

Professor Brian Webster-Henderson
Dean of Learning and Teaching, Professor of Nursing, Edinburgh Napier University
Brian Webster-Henderson has a lengthy career in education, specialising first as a mental health nurse in the areas of alcohol and drug addiction and then as a general nurse working in emergency medicine. Since his move into academia he has specialised on the pedagogical aspects of education, always placing a strong focus on the importance of communication through teaching, and maintaining a student-centred perspective. He maintains strong ties with his nursing career, speaking often on the topic of nursing education.

References

Barnett, R. (2000). *Realising the University in an Age of Supercomplexity.* Buckingham: Open University Press.

Clark, E. and Webster, B. (2012). Innovation and its contribution to the scholarship of learning and teaching. *Nurse Education Today,* 32 (7), 729–731.

1

Importing new philosophies into course design

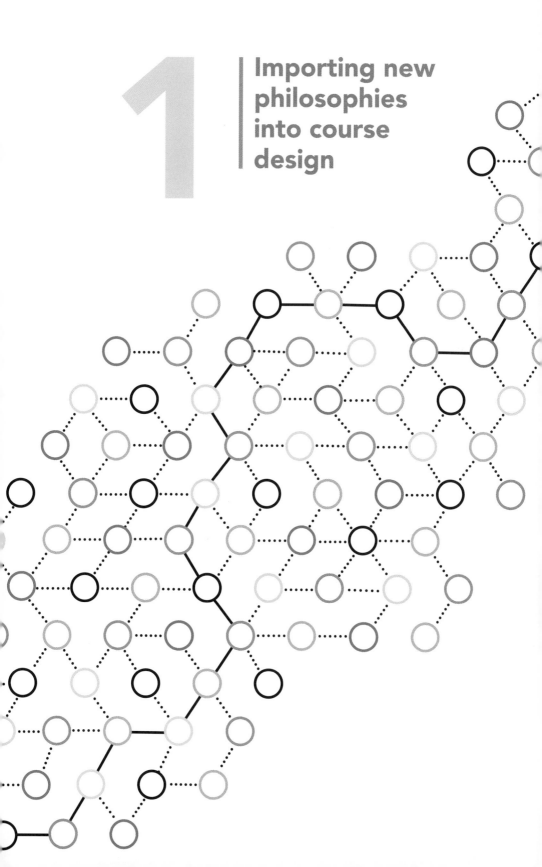

Innovation and entrepreneurship: learning lessons in uncertainty

Richard Whitecross

ABSTRACT

What does it mean to teach innovation and entrepreneurship in professional degrees? Professions such as accountancy and law traditionally provide specialised knowledge and advice. As technology makes the professional's knowledge more accessible, professions need to innovate. This chapter outlines the use of an innovative challenge to teach final year LLB (Bachelor of Laws) students about innovation and entrepreneurship, combining academic theory with practical experience in conceptualising an innovative service (the challenge) for law firms, and in pitching to a panel of professionals. For the group involved, the encounter with working professionals raised a range of concerns. How would the students engage with the challenge and cope with the experience of direct, immediate feedback on their ideas and work?

Drawing on student self-reflection, and feedback of the professional panel and observers, this chapter highlights how failing and dealing with practical challenges as a lecturer, and co-creating the course, can enrich the experience of lecturer and student. It contributes to academic practice by illustrating how stretching the existing paradigms of pedagogic tradition can enable students to develop skills in a safe, supportive environment in which constructive critical challenges are accepted and valued.

Keywords: profession, innovation, uncertainty, growth

Introduction

In the UK LLB [...] we still, on the whole, [...] have little impact on and almost no input to professional educational initiatives (Maharg, 2007, p.4).

What does it mean to teach innovation and entrepreneurship in the context of undergraduate profession-focused programmes? Maharg, writing just before the 2008 recession, states that "many of our twenty-first century law schools still inhabit an industrial system of education inherited from a twentieth century mired in nineteenth-century structures" (2007, p.5). In Scotland, major law firms have disappeared and new firms have emerged.[1] Clients expect more from the professional (Susskind and Susskind, 2015). Should professional education not reflect changes in the delivery of professional services? If so, how? Interviewing leading professionals working in major accountancy and law firms in Scotland, a key theme emerged that challenges traditional approaches to teaching undergraduate professional-entrance degrees. Specifically, the professionals interviewed commented on the need for students to be innovative and entrepreneurial. Universities play an important part in national economies, and there is strong evidence that university students who engage in entrepreneurial programmes are more likely to "secure jobs more quickly", and are "more confident in their abilities to innovate in the workplace and start new business" than their peers (Johnson et al., 2016, p.8). Moreland specifically makes the link between entrepreneurship and innovation, noting that "a distinctive feature is the recognition that while entrepreneurship often shows up in the form of self-employment, it can also take the form of innovative and creative activity by employees in larger enterprises" (2004, p.2). Moreland importantly states that "it is a mistake to see entrepreneurship as an add-on, offered to a few" (ibid). This chapter builds and extends our consideration of introducing and supporting students as they learn about innovation and entrepreneurship beyond modules that specifically teach these subjects. Drawing on the experience of final year law students studying an optional Honours level module, this chapter argues that in working with students we can, irrespective of our discipline, support their understanding of innovation and enterprise as part of the wider skillset developed during their university careers (Keogh and Galloway, 2004; Moreland, 2004).

In 1996, a central recommendation of the Lord Chancellor's Advisory Committee on Legal Education and Conduct's *First Report on Legal Education and Training* was that "the degree course should stand as an independent liberal education in the discipline of law, not tied to any specific vocation" (1996, p.5). Seventeen years later, the Legal Education and Training Review (2013) raised deep concerns over professional values and the absence of entrepreneurship in law degrees. This oscillation in views on the purpose of the law degree is important for our discussion of how to teach innovation and entrepreneurship. How indeed, when there is no agreement, nor any competing claims on what the LLB degree should contain or seek to do in terms of preparing the student for a life in the legal profession.

It is generally acknowledged that the Law Society of Scotland views the LLB degree as providing a liberal education rather than as a vocational degree.

This chapter argues that irrespective of whether or not the LLB is a liberal education or a vocational degree, there is a need to consider what is meant by professional values and commercial awareness, as part of the broader skillset we aim to provide for the development of our students.

This chapter outlines a new approach to teaching final year LLB students about innovation and entrepreneurship, combining academic theory with practical experience in conceptualising an innovative new service for law firms, and in pitching to a panel of professionals. Drawing on student self-reflection, on professional comments, and on feedback, this chapter shows how dealing with uncertainty by attempting the unfamiliar can enrich the learning for lecturer and student alike.

The chapter is set out in five sections. Section one outlines the context and rationale for developing the module and, in particular, the Innovation Challenge. The challenges and contradictions faced within the profession are discussed at some length, for it is important that we place the approach discussed later in the chapter in the broader context of the relationship between professional bodies, as they set entry requirements and university structures. In section two the Innovation Challenge is outlined and set in the wider context of the module. The following section draws on feedback from students, professional participants, and other observers. It focuses on what the students learned from the experience. Section four considers the key lessons, notably that the students reported the experience as empowering. Finally, section five concludes the chapter with an argument for building an element of formative assessment into appropriate modules, irrespective of subject, providing the students with feedback to reflect on.

The missing elements: innovation and entrepreneurship

In June 2013, the *Legal Education and Training Review* (LETR) was published. LETR focuses on legal education and provision in England and Wales. However, it is relevant to – and will influence – legal education teaching in Scotland. Among a range of concerns, the review identified the lack of educational provision on entrepreneurship in the undergraduate LLB degree. LETR highlighted the gap even in the qualification stages of training. LETR noted that commercial awareness was often mentioned as a skill that is often lacking in young lawyers (see figure 1). However, no specific proposals on how to address a lack of entrepreneurship or commercial awareness were offered. At present, the focus of the undergraduate LLB is on the substantial areas of law and the production of legal knowledge.

Legal Education and Training Review Chapter Two

Professional knowledge

2.70 Two areas are also often mentioned as lacking among new recruits in interviews and focus groups: ethics/professionalism and "commercial awareness".

Commercial awareness

2.74 In the online survey 68.9% of practitioners indicated that knowledge of the business context is important or very important to their work, ranking it above a number of areas of core legal knowledge. This emphasis on commercial awareness in training has been a recurrent finding in the research [...] Although this is considered by many respondents to be a significant deficiency in new recruits, the nature of the deficiency is not always clearly articulated, and respondents were divided on when that deficit (whatever it is) should be addressed.

2.75 The careers advisers' survey offers some assistance on what, from their experience, employers are looking for when they talk about commercial awareness. This suggests that commercial awareness is a composite concept that may comprise a broad body of knowledge, as well as a number of associated skills and attributes:

- awareness of the sector and the clients' business; having an interest in the sector so as to be able to communicate with clients;
- appreciation of law as a business: that firms (etc.) are profit-making entities; marketing and networking; how law firms are run;
- an ability to recognise clients' commercial objectives rather than proposing *pure law* solutions;
- wider knowledge of commercial and financial subjects: understanding financial products; corporate structures; markets and sectors; knowledge of the wider economic environment and business issues in the news;
- general knowledge of current world and political affairs;
- numeracy and ability to interpret financial data; office skills and use of specific tools such as Microsoft Excel;
- personal attributes of common sense, independent thinking; critical thinking – not accepting views or approaches at face value.

Figure 1: LETR Report 2013 (pp.35–36) – Professionalism and commercial awareness.

In Scotland, following a review of legal education, the postgraduate Diploma in Legal Practice currently provides the main introduction to core professional skills. Therefore, following LETR, there is a similar need to consider how we teach students about professional conduct, and about being innovative during the undergraduate LLB. As indicated in figure 1, what is meant by commercial awareness or innovation in the Scottish legal educational context is open to a range of interpretations and perspectives, which impact on the teaching of these core attributes of the professional lawyer. Certainly, as touched on previously, there is a general view that the LLB should not be concerned with these considerations. However, this chapter argues that if we are to support our students' wider personal and professional development, then we should provide them with opportunities that stretch and challenge. In turn, this should build on growing empirical evidence that students who learn about innovation and entrepreneurship have significantly improved graduate employment opportunities (Oosterbeek, van Praag and Ijsselstein, 2010).

There is a growing literature critical of the role of law schools, notably in the US, for their failure to support the development of an "ethos of professionalism among law students" (Montgomery, 2008, p.338). It is striking how critical academic literature is of legal education and of its failure to engage with developing professionalism. It is argued that in both substance and pedagogy the predominant emphasis in law schools is on analytical skills and reasoning, through broad exposure to a range of legal areas. A survey of law texts aimed at undergraduate law students quickly demonstrates the importance placed on critical reading and legal reasoning. However, there is less emphasis on the wider ongoing development of a professional ethos, with even less, if any at all, on innovation and entrepreneurship. It is worth noting that a distinction is being made between teaching about the law in relation to intellectual property or innovations, and lawyers being capable of being innovative and entrepreneurial in business.

After over 50 site visits across the US to study how professional schools educate lawyers, doctors, engineers, and nurses, the president of the Carnegie Foundation for the Advancement of Teaching, Lee Shulman, noted that: "the most overlooked aspect of professional preparation was the formation of a professional identity," (Shulman, 2010, p.ix) around which the student was taught. In 2007, the Carnegie Foundation published *Educating Lawyers* (Sullivan et al., 2007). It argues that legal education needs a more integrated, holistic approach towards educating lawyers. To do this there is a need to elevate education for practice and professional identity to the same level as education for legal analysis. In the same year, a report by the Clinical Legal Education Association, *Best Practices for Legal Education* (Stuckey, 2007) emphasised the importance of teaching practice and professionalism at the centre of legal education.

In a general review of legal writing on professionalism and legal pedagogy, Montgomery (2008, p.323) summarises the general view presented by legal writers: "Law schools are inadequately developing an ethos of professionalism in law students". Concerns over the lack of legal teaching focused on legal professionalism appear to be cyclical. In Scotland we can see it in discussions over the Diploma and recent changes to its structure. Yet, despite the changes, there remain consistent criticisms of the perceived lack of understanding of the importance of innovation among law graduates.[2] It is against this broader context of concerns over professionalism that the focus on the apparent absence of innovation and entrepreneurialism in professional degrees is set.

Introducing innovation and entrepreneurship

In September 2014 a new final year Honours module was introduced to the LLB (Honours) options of students at this Scottish University. The module was developed in response to the publication of LETR in 2013. However, a key driver for the new module was work undertaken by the module leader with a number of Scottish law firms, focusing on the changing landscape of legal services and client expectations in 2013–14. During this period, the practical challenges of the Scottish legal sector were highlighted by the demise of long-established major law firms. A key absence was an understanding of broader business principles and, in particular, of the relevance of innovation and entrepreneurship in the context of professional-service firms.

After piloting the module in autumn 2014, the module leader identified the need for an opportunity for students to put into practice key elements of the module: an innovation challenge. How could this be constructively and meaningfully integrated into the module? At present, the core law modules present doctrinal law rather than experience or insight to the wider considerations needed in running a legal practice. These same skills apply beyond the legal profession.

Preparing for the Innovation Challenge

Following an interview about the importance of innovation and enterprise in law teaching, an opportunity arose that allowed the lecturer to move his thinking forward, and to adapt the module assessment strategy to apply learning in a new and challenging way. Building on research insights and working in close collaboration with colleagues from Careers and the Scottish Institute for Enterprise, a bespoke Innovation Challenge was designed.

During the ten weeks leading up to the Innovation Challenge, the students were allocated groups to prepare an assessed group presentation. Each group had four students. The allocation of the groups was made by the module leader and sought to ensure that the students worked outside of their normal social circle. Each group was set the same brief:

The Group Presentation Brief

As you are aware, the firm needs to consider its future direction. You and your colleagues are invited to present to a selected panel of senior partners on Thursday 30 October.

At the meeting, the senior partners will be looking for ideas to fulfil the brief.

The brief is: "The firm recognises that it needs to address changes to legal services. How can the firm retain or improve its current position and develop its client service offering?"

You must come to the meeting prepared with your ideas in a ten-minute presentation. The senior partners will then expect you to be able to answer questions on your presentation.

The purpose of the group presentation is explained in the assessment brief as seeking to:

- provide students with experience of working in a team towards a clear goal: the presentation;
- provide students with the opportunity to learn about different working styles and how to accommodate these in a team;
- provide students with the opportunity to discuss new ideas, be creative, and deepen their learning;
- receive feedback on the group presentation to support future presentations by the students (either individually or as part of a group).

The students were asked to incorporate and consider key themes discussed in-seminar about strategy in professional-service firms, talent management, client relationship and the importance of innovation in relation to client services. As part of the preparation of the students for the group presentation, a bespoke workshop on team dynamics and personalities was developed and delivered by colleagues from Careers. The students were resistant to being allocated groups, and found the early stages of working together challenging. In feedback, a student noted:

I was dead sceptical about the workshop. Did not want to do it. But really learned a lot from it [...]. It made me understand not only the others but me.

The workshop provided them with valuable insights into their own preferred working styles and those of their colleagues (Barton and Westwood, 2006).

The students discussed their learning from the assignment in their post-presentation reflective account, to varying degrees of depth. In the more reflective pieces there was evidence of the students taking time to stand back and discuss the learning achieved through the preparation and delivery of the group presentation. Importantly, they viewed the group presentation as presenting a range of challenges in terms of working in groups, being creative, and observing time management skills. From a teaching perspective an interesting observation was watching how students discussed their perceived failures. These included being unwilling to challenge colleagues, being reluctant to voice or push their ideas and suggestions, and feeling unable to speak confidently when presenting to the class and members of staff. Some students commented on how the presentation either made them look forward to the Innovation Challenge or increased their anxiety about it, even though it was not part of the formal assessment.

The Innovation Challenge

The Innovation Challenge was designed to draw together the themes considered in the module seminars and to build on the experience gained from learning to work with other students on the group presentation (Blasi, 1995). The idea for the Innovation Challenge emerged out of seminar discussions with the module students, who expressed a desire to apply what they were learning. In addition, the lecturer was working with 15 final year students on how to advise creative industry students developing innovative new products. The Innovation Challenge grew from these experiences and from student feedback during the course of the trimester. Responding to students' interest and following discussions with the Dean of the Business School, subject group lead, other academic colleagues and the students on the module, the lecturer agreed to hold an Innovation Challenge. This was not assessed, and participation was not mandatory. This was a new development reflecting a process of co-creation between the lecturer and the students. However, because the Innovation Challenge builds on learning on the module, participation was restricted to students enrolled on the module.

With the agreement of the students, the Innovation Challenge was scheduled to take place three weeks after the group presentation to allow time for formative feedback. The students were advised that they would be presented a scenario and set a challenge to design and present a commercial, innovative pitch to a panel of judges during a three-hour session. The panel of judges was composed of three commercial lawyers in private practice with major Scottish law firms. The fourth judge was a man with experience of start-ups. No additional information on the nature of the challenge was provided, and students were advised that there was no prior preparation required. However, they were asked to dress appropriately for a professional context.

On the day of the Innovation Challenge, the students were allocated to new groups at tables spaced across the room. Each table was provided with a range of materials that included coloured pens, Post-its, A3 paper, and a stand. On arrival, students were asked to join their table and to decide on a name for their group.

The Innovation Challenge was introduced by a video that was based on interviews with a range of individuals (a general practitioner, a consultant specialising in dementia, a carer, and a representative from a charity, who talked about dementia and the practical day-to-day issues arising from it). The film set out the context of this serious social issue, of which the students had varying levels of knowledge and understanding. Some students, for example, were studying medical law and were aware of some of the legal issues that arise from dementia, while other students may have had some experience in their family. Following the video, the facilitator (an experienced private-sector lawyer) led a discussion with the students about issues that arose from the film. It was only after this initial discussion that the students were explained what their Innovation Challenge would be.

The Innovation Challenge was to identify and design either a legal service or a product addressing some of the issues outlined in the video. The students were allocated 90 minutes to complete the task before presenting their innovation pitch to the panel of four judges. During the time given, the lecturer circulated among the groups listening as they worked through the process of considering possible innovations, tested their options, and refined their choices. When designing the challenge, it was agreed that the lecturer should not take an active part in the development of the concepts. Instead the facilitator, who had experience in working with entrepreneurs, provided each group with critical feedback and challenged their initial ideas and suggestions.

On reflection the lecturer noted that the facilitator was probably more challenging to the students than the lecturer would have been. Importantly, and as observed by the facilitator and two observers, the students struggled with the lecturer's non-active role. When he was asked questions by students it was clear that they expected or wanted him to provide them with direction. As a result, the lecturer personally found the 90 minutes challenging and unsettling. Writing after the event, he commented: "I found myself worrying about a range of issues that I could not control. What if it was too much for them?"

At the end of the strictly-timed session, the students were required to prepare a presentation for their proposed innovation. At the close of this second part of the session, the judges were introduced to the students. Three of them were female senior lawyers from prominent law firms, and each briefly explained their individual backgrounds. The only male judge, a non-lawyer, introduced himself and his experience of working with student business start-ups. Each group of students was then invited to present to the panel for five minutes, and to answer questions for three minutes. Each group was allowed to choose whether or not to use the stand to present their illustrative diagrams or the bullet-pointed details of their innovation. Time was strictly monitored and each presentation was stopped at the end of five minutes. Similarly, the judges' questions were strictly timed.

On completion of all five presentations, the judges were invited to discuss the pitches and to choose one winner. The judges chose not to leave the room and remained visible as they discretely discussed each of the five presentations. After 20 minutes, the judges indicated that they were in a position to name the winner and to provide feedback. They commented on each pitch individually in order of presentation, and highlighted strengths and weaknesses as appropriate. The winning group was announced and the judges took time to commend the runners-up.

Reflecting on the Innovation Challenge: learning and impact

The Innovation Challenge was new. It arose from collaboration with the students. From the lecturer's perspective, it was untested. The lecturer was unsure how it would be received by the students, with this uncertainty causing him to appreciate and empathise with the many emotions they experienced. It provided an opportunity for situated learning in a different learning environment (Brown, Collins and Duguid, 1989). Since it was developed during term time, the challenge could not be part of the formal assessment of the module. As a result, a number of students did not show on the day of the challenge. Some were ill, while others simply chose not to attend or provide an explanation for not attending. This was disappointing and frustrating. However, although about a quarter of the class did not participate, the feedback from the students who attended was constructive and positive. It is worth noting that one student, who had indicated that she would have to leave early, commented that she was "really glad to have stayed". At the end of the event, students were invited to reflect on the process to provide feedback. We provided them with four questions, written on four separate A3 sheets on the wall near the exit door, and asked them to answer them anonymously on Post-its:

- How did you feel before the challenge began?
- What did you think of the challenge given to your team?
- What did you learn?
- What will you do to build on the experience?

The majority of students were anxious about the challenge. They did not know what to expect and were particularly concerned about the external judges' perceptions of them. Uncertainty about what they would be asked to do, who they would be working with, and what "innovation" might "look like" were common responses. Students commented specifically on the lecturer's presence and role as being less active than they expected.

The challenge surprised a number of students, who were not expecting "such a practical issue". There was an expectation that the challenge would be more business-heavy. However, several students studying mental health law found it interesting, recognising that it presented a range of opportunities for law firms. The DVD of interviews, and the practical information provided in a relatively short space of time, were considered effective. Several noted that it made them more aware of the importance of making broader connections about current issues. One aspect of the challenge which the majority of the students commented on was the level of challenge presented to them by the facilitator. This can be illustrated by two comments made to the lecturer during this phase:

"She asked, 'How will that actually work?' We did not know!"

and

"She said our idea was not very original."

The directness of the facilitator surprised the students. However, since the facilitator's comments were addressed to the group rather than to one individual, the students afterwards reported that they felt they were able to respond to the comments and to take them on board in a constructive manner. One student observed that because the facilitator treated them as her equals, her directness was appropriate, and a good example for those who had previously felt unable to speak up.

"I learned that I am entrepreneurial!" This comment was put forward by another student, who noted that "although dreading the challenge, I have learned that I can be innovative". Many of the comments focused on group work, and the value of building on the earlier experience of group work and presentations. Others noted that although they had been "upfront" with their group, they had personally contributed little during the pitch or "had too much to say". As a result, a significant number of students identified presentation skills as an area for future development. Exploring student concerns about presentations in a subsequent seminar, confidence was identified as the key element that they lacked. It is important to add that there were limitations with the feedback received and the manner it was gathered. Responses to the final two questions tended to blur. This was very clear, as the Post-its were all on the A3 sheet for question three (what did you learn?). This probably reflects the nature of the experience and the need to consider more carefully how student feedback is sought.

It is worth noting that, although the Innovation Challenge was not assessed, the students who participated viewed it as an important part of their module studies. The experience was viewed as formative, as it allowed them to explore ideas and to be creative with fellow students they did not normally work with. Equally, the experience was viewed as good practice for some forms of assessment centre used by law firms to help with their trainee selection process. In particular, the students found on reflection that negotiating their relationship and interaction with the facilitator made them conscious of how important it was to consider their own professional demeanour. Finally, the majority of the students thought that the challenge drew the various themes of the module together in a practical and exciting – if daunting – manner.

Engaging with the professionals

One week after the Innovation Challenge, the whole class attended a workshop at a major Edinburgh law firm. The session was led by the managing partner, the chief operating officer, several partners, and six trainee lawyers. The workshop focused on how a major law firm operates, how it approaches developing and implementing its business strategy and, importantly, the creation of a new innovation unit. One of the judges from the Innovation Challenge was present, and provided further informal feedback to the class. Significantly, the judge invited the runners-up to present their proposal to a number of her colleagues who were interested in it. The participants in the Innovation Challenge posed several difficult questions to the Managing Partner. In feedback from the firm, it was noted that the quality of the questions raised reflected an unusual understanding of the challenges facing professional-service firms.

Going forward: some thoughts for practice

Innovation and entrepreneurship need not be a missing element of undergraduate courses (Moreland, 2004). After piloting the Innovation Challenge, it is evident that students benefit from being asked to address an issue and to receive constructive, robust feedback. As the judges strongly iterated, they were impressed by the quality of the ideas and presentations. However, they also indicated areas to work on. In turn, the feedback from students on their experience and learning from the challenge, together with the feedback from the judges and the observers, have identified new areas to be considered in the module.

We can all, irrespective of our discipline, consider how to introduce our students to the practice of being innovative. Reflection on the experience of the students, and on their comments that they should be "learning this earlier," suggests that we should look at how we can incrementally introduce and develop our students' understanding of innovation and, by extension, entrepreneurship. Building on the Innovation Challenge, we can consider imaginative ways of gradually embedding innovation into our modules and programmes. Students value the experience of applying their learning. Presenting a challenge from the social world around them and inviting them to approach it from a different perspective can be unpredictable and even daunting for both lecturer and student.

As Keogh and Galloway (2004) highlight, the positive experience of engaging in innovation builds student confidence. Crucially, Badii and Sharif (2003) and Keogh and Galloway (2004) all demonstrate that there is a need for innovation and enterprise to be integrated into university education. This requires a planned and integrated approach across subject groups and beyond. It requires teachers to step outside of their own areas of practice and to work collaboratively with others, mirroring the behaviours and skills we want our students to develop. Students benefit from the opportunity to develop their understanding of the practical issues that face businesses, and to learn about the importance of innovation, creativity and entrepreneurship. The Innovation Challenge is not a new concept in itself, building as it does on popular television programmes such as *Dragon's Den* and *The Apprentice*. What *is* new is explicitly providing a valuable learning experience to students who otherwise would not have an opportunity to think about innovation and entrepreneurship. Importantly, the Innovation Challenge taught the students that they are capable of being innovative and entrepreneurial.

Dr Richard Whitecross, Lecturer in Law, holds degrees in History, Law, and Social Anthropology. He was awarded his PhD in 2002 by the University of Edinburgh where he was an ESRC Postdoctoral Fellow, Lecturer in Social Anthropology and ESRC Research Fellow, before joining the Civil Service in 2007. In 2012 Richard joined Edinburgh Napier University, where he has designed innovative law and professional practice modules. He is a member of the Steering Committee of the Legal Education Research Network. In 2014, he was awarded HEA Law Strategic Project funding. Richard is a Senior Fellow of the HEA and an ESRC Peer Review College member.

Notes

1. In May 2014, Dundas and Wilson, one of the oldest and largest Scottish law firms, merged with CMS Cameron McKenna. The takeover was completed in December 2015.
2. During a major conference on Series B Investment (26 November 2015) organised by MBM Commercial, the author spoke with a number of leading commercial lawyers, chartered accountants, and entrepreneurs about the importance of innovation and the implications for the professions.

References

Badii, A. and Sharif, A. (2003). Information management and knowledge integration for enterprise innovation. *Logistics Information Management,* 16 (2), 145–155.

Barton, K. and Westwood, F. (2006). From student to trainee practitioner – a study of team working as a learning experience. *Web Journal of Current Legal Issues,* (3), 1–15.

Blasi, G. (1995). What lawyers know: lawyering expertise, cognitive science and the functions of theory. *Journal of Legal Education,* 45 (3), 313–397.

Brown, J. S., Collins, A. and Duguid, P. (1989). Situated cognition and the culture of learning. *Educational Researcher,* 18 (1), 32–42.

Johnson, L., Adams Becker, S., Cummins, M., Estrada, V., Freeman, A. and Hall, C. (2016). *NMC Horizon Report: 2016 Higher Education Edition.* Austin, Texas: The New Media Consortium.

Keogh, W. and Galloway, L. (2004). Teaching enterprise in vocational disciplines: reflecting on positive experience. *Management Decisions,* 42 (3/4), 531–541

Legal Education and Training Review (2013). *Setting Standards: The Future of Legal Services Education and Training Regulation in England and Wales*

[Online]. Available at: http://letr.org.uk/the-report/index.html [Accessed 1 April 2016].

Lord Chancellor's Advisory Committee on Legal Education and Conduct (1996). *First Report on Legal Education and Training.* London: ACLEC.

Maharg, P. (2007). *Transforming Legal Education: Learning and Teaching the Law in the Early Twenty-first Century.* Aldershot: Ashgate Publishing Ltd.

Montgomery, J. (2008). Incorporating emotional intelligence concepts into legal education: strengthening the professionalism of law students. *University of Toledo Law Review,* (39), 323–352

Moreland, N. (2004). *Entrepreneurship and Higher Education: An Employability Perspective.* Higher Education Authority [Online]. Available at: https://www.heacademy.ac.uk/sites/default/files/id461_entrepreneurship_and_higher_education_341.pdf [Accessed 1 April 2016].

Oosterbeek, H., van Praag, M. and Ijsselstein, A. (2010). The impact of entrepreneurship education on entrepreneurship skills and motivation. *European Economic Review,* 54 (3), 442–454.

Shulman, L. (2010). "Foreword" in Cooke M. et al., *Educating Physicians: A Call for Reform of Medical School and Residency.* San Francisco: Jossey-Bass.

Stuckey, R. (2007). *Best Practices for Legal Education.* University Publications, University of South Carolina: Clinical Legal Education Association.

Sullivan, W. M., Colby, A., Welch Wegner, J., Bond, L. and Shulman, L. S. (2007). *Educating Lawyers: Preparation for the Profession of Law.* Jossey-Bass: Carnegie Foundation.

Susskind, R. and Susskind, D. (2015). *The Future of the Professions: How Technology Will Transform the Work of Human Experts.* Oxford: Oxford University Press.

Autonomous student learning: the value of a Finnish approach

Isla Kapasi

ABSTRACT

Existing entrepreneurship education delivery within Higher Education Institutions (HEIs) is not meeting the needs of employers. It appears that a focus on learning about entrepreneurship via simulation methods builds knowledge and skills, but does not in fact support the development of autonomous and self-directed learners. In contrast, this conceptual chapter explores an innovative Finnish methodology of entrepreneurship education based on autonomous and self-determined learning. In Team Academy (TA) students learn about entrepreneurship *through* entrepreneurship. To do this, students create their own team business supported by coaches. Key to the approach is that the businesses trade in the open market and responsibility, ownership, and control for the business and for learning rest with the students. The contribution of the TA approach to entrepreneurship education in UK HEIs, with particular reference to theories of learning and entrepreneurship – heutagogy and effectuation respectively – is considered. In addition, implications for practice in the HEI context, such as the use of learning contracts and the coaching method of teaching facilitation, are explored.

Keywords: heutagogy, team entrepreneurship, self-determined learning

Introduction

Sarason comments that to "produce responsible, self-sufficient citizens who possess the self-esteem, initiative, skills, and wisdom to continue individual growth and pursue knowledge" (1990, p.163) is the essential purpose of education. This purpose would underpin many educational approaches such as pedagogy. However, education in the HEI context not only seeks to impart knowledge and skills to learners, but to encourage them to be lifelong learners. This represents a shift from pedagogy to self-directed learning (SDL). Knowles developed the concept of SDL and described it as "a process in which individuals take the initiative, with or without the help of others, in diagnosing their learning needs, formulating learning goals, identifying human and material resources, choosing and implementing appropriate learning strategies, and evaluating learning outcomes" (1975, p.18). According to Dynan et al. (2008), SDL is a skill which can be acquired, requiring that learners take active personal involvement, ownership, and control of their learning and have a measure of self-awareness (also Roberson Jr., 2005; Silén and Uhlin, 2008; Canning, 2010).

The value of engaging in SDL has been examined in a variety of educational contexts. For example, Bhoyrub et al. consider the importance of the learning approach within nursing. They find that student nurses are required to engage in "reflexive learner reactions" (2010, p.323) in order to be able to integrate new experiences with their prior learning in a complex and ever-changing environment. Similar discoveries were found in work with students with disabilities (Wehmeyer et al., 2000), mature learners (Canning, 2010), older adults (Roberson Jr., 2005), medical students (Bhat et al., 2007), and university students in the UK (Bramhall et al., 2008; Scott, 2010). However, whilst knowledge and skills underpinned by a teacher-supported SDL approach to learning are important (Silén and Uhlin, 2008; Jossberger et al., 2010), complex and changing environments require today's HEI students to take ownership and control of their (lifelong) learning. This is as true for entrepreneurship education as it is of any other.

At both political and university level, entrepreneurship education is considered crucial (Henry et al., 2005). This is the case not only for the individual student in terms of the flexibility and adaptability demanded by the labour market, but for the wider economy in terms of growth and jobs creation (QAA, 2012; Hoppe, 2016). Research suggests that entrepreneurship education activities are transdisciplinary and contribute to "employability, innovation, knowledge transfer, commercialization, and intellectual property" (QAA, 2012, p.2). Thus, the value of entrepreneurship education for individuals and the economy is largely accepted, yet the method of entrepreneurship education delivery and its underlying pedagogy have been the subject of continued scrutiny (for example, Tosey et al., 2013; Hoppe, 2016). There are many different approaches to embedding entrepreneurship education within curricula – whether that be via specific courses or integrated alongside other Higher Education (HE) programmes. However, within the United Kingdom, the majority of entrepreneurship education courses focus on education about entrepreneurship, and simulations of entrepreneurship activity. Yet one of the key messages that emerges from education and industry bodies is that employers expect graduates to have a "business-ready mindset" (Association of Business Schools et al., 2014, p.5) which has not been evident in recent graduates. To this end, practice-based pedagogical tools are recommended to equip students with the skills, knowledge, communication, self-awareness, people-management, and problem-solving abilities of a desirable graduate. We now turn to Team Academy: a specific practice-based approach of entrepreneurship education.

TA is an innovative methodology of entrepreneurship education and learning *through* entrepreneurship, established in Finland over the past 20 years. TA has been described as innovative by Tosey et al. (2013) because it deviates from existing practice within many HEI business schools worldwide. Thus, based on the concerns of education and industry bodies, the TA approach could address the gap in existing entrepreneurship education of educating *about* and *for* by allowing students to engage in first-hand experiences of entrepreneurship.

This chapter further explores the learning activities, context, and teaching at a TA programme operated by Tampere University of Applied Sciences (TAMK), which is called Pro Akatemia. Pro Akatemia is an offshoot of the original TA programme developed in Jyväskylä, Finland. It has its own unique approach to implementing the TA methodology; in some ways the approach has been replicated, whereas in others it has changed based on the delivery environment and culture of TAMK. Participation in a Tampere learning expedition by the author has raised several issues for consideration with regards to the existing delivery of entrepreneurial education within the authors' home institution, and beyond that, to understand the TA approach as a fundamentally different learning approach for entrepreneurship education. Of principal interest is the importance of autonomous and self-determined learning: the foundation of the TA approach. While this is not a new approach in some areas of UK HEI delivery (for example, Bramhall et al., 2008; Scott, 2010), it is underdeveloped in entrepreneurship education and within the UK HEI landscape generally. Therefore, as per Jones et al. (2014), who call for a new language to describe what entrepreneurship education does, this chapter contributes to that developing area by theoretically examining a learning approach which can underpin the applied aspects of entrepreneurial education. Furthermore, it outlines an applied programme approach – TA – which sets out a method to deliver a new -*gogy* of learning in an HEI.

The remaining sections of this chapter address the learning approach, or *heutagogy*, underpinning TA, how this might fit with an effectuation, a process theory of entrepreneurship, and how (and if) this learning *through* entrepreneurship can be implemented in a UK HEI. The chapter concludes with several key TA approach features that may be transferable beyond its entrepreneurship education framework.

Team Academy

Team Academy is an approach to entrepreneurship education originating from Jyväskylä, Finland. Developed by Johannes Partenen over 20 years ago, the approach is underpinned by his philosophy that individuals learn in social settings when they apply theory to practice. The core educational purpose of TA is to equip individuals to be able to cope in uncertain life situations. Therefore, no longer is there a focus on training for (specific) jobs, but instead on facilitating individuals in their self-determined learning so that they can manage unknown situations and occupations, either on their own or as employees. The approach is ultimately about learning how to learn and how to be adaptable. The approach for entrepreneurship education delivery is underpinned by the TA manifesto of five principles:

1. Societies can be made dynamic through team entrepreneurship. Team entrepreneurs are development engines that will force society to change.
2. Structures must be created to help small businesses network internationally. Inspiration and enthusiasm are generated by the power of self-organisation.
3. Team entrepreneurs have taken responsibility for their own lives, and they continually strive for excellence. Team entrepreneurs learn in practice and by reading a lot.
4. Team entrepreneurs see things that no one else can see yet. Vision leads to something new, and belief in the vision is so strong that it becomes reality.
5. Team entrepreneurs play fairly with other entrepreneurs and fulfil all their obligations to their own immediate environment and society with integrity.

To this end, in a HEI environment, TA students create their own team (profit-oriented) business from which all of their learning emerges. There are two key pedagogic values; first, that the students learn by *doing*, and second, that they do so by working co-operatively within a team. Consequently, students on the programme are referred to as Team Entrepreneurs (TEs). Entry into the programme can happen at different stages. For example, in Jyväskylä, students commence their TA studies immediately in year one (equivalent to level seven in Scotland), whereas in Tampere, Finland, students join the programme in year two: usually after a general business studies foundation year.

Teams are established when the student enters into the programme, formed based on psychological testing conducted in the pre-induction stage to create coherent and balanced teams. Teams are large and can include up to 20 students. In the early stages, teams select their business or team name to establish their identity throughout their time on the programme. Within the large team, various operating arrangements are possible. First, for the purposes of running the large team, TEs hold leadership or management responsibilities such as managing finances or human resources. However, the TEs are not restricted to working only as one large team. Consequently, small sub-teams with discrete business ideas may emerge. Thus, the large team may run a whole-team business, but there may also be several other smaller businesses run under the larger team body; essentially, they operate in a similar way to a holding company. Nonetheless, whatever the team operating approach, all monies generated as part of team activity contribute to the larger team pot. Teams can decide what to do with their income: for example, they may save it for international travel (strongly recommended at TA) or they may choose to take a salary. It is worth noting that all businesses created are owned exclusively by the TEs. This means that both gains and risk are their responsibility.

In addition to learning from their peers, students are supported by a team coach. Team coaches do not take on the role of teacher or lecturer; rather, they are specially trained in Team Mastery coaching skills to facilitate the TEs and their learning. Nevertheless, they may be employed as teachers or lecturers or be practicing business people in their other roles. The purpose of the team coach is to coach and support the students as individuals or in their teams, and also to facilitate their activities. Coaches do not provide materials, lead sessions or arrange events; the students are entirely self-determined and self-supporting. For example, learners set the parameters on what they do; they decide if they have completed a piece of coursework or module component appropriately. To summarise, from the process of operating a business, working in teams, confronting failures, celebrating successes, and taking self-responsibility, the TEs learn how to learn and become adaptable to new, unfamiliar environments.

To give some further context about TA, the programme currently operates in ten countries worldwide (Finland, the United Kingdom, Spain, Australia, Netherlands, Brazil, France, Hungary, Argentina, and China). At the most recent count, 10,000 people have passed through the method and in 2015 there were 1,300 TEs supported by 800 team coaches. The approach also boasts some impressive statistics, both for business success measures and measures important to a university. For example, at Jyväskylä University of Applied Sciences (the home university of the TA programme) in 2012, TEs (180 supported by eight team coaches) had a turnover of over €2 million. In addition, two years after graduation, 47 per cent of TEs were operating their own business. However, it is worth noting that the Finnish context may be a distinct contributory factor to these outcomes. For example, education remains free for every citizen in Finland, and is funded by the government for up to seven years. Furthermore, Finnish universities are measured on the employment status of students after graduation and the duration in which a student completes their degree (that is, how quickly the student moves through the system). TA scores well on both measures. Notably from the Tampere learning expedition trip many of the students on the TA course were mature by UK standards (in their mid-twenties).

As previously mentioned, the TA approach has been applied at several UK HEIs, including: Northumbria University, University of the West of England (UWE), University of Westminster, Falmouth University, and Bishop Grosseteste University in Lincoln. This year, two institutions have students who will be the first UK HEI cohorts to graduate from a three-year degree programme (Northumbria University and UWE). From additional learning expeditions to the UK institutions, it appears that these organisations take the key tenets of TA and create their own TA micro-culture (Tosey et al., 2013). This suggests that the TA approach has value for a UK context, yet adjustment has been required. Therefore, how does TA fit within a traditional UK HEI pedagogical approach used for delivery of entrepreneurship education? What does this mean for entrepreneurship education in general? What does it mean for the delivery of learning across HEIs? The learning theory underpinning the TA approach, followed by theory specific to the entrepreneurship process, is now detailed.

Heutagogy and effectuation theory

There are several differences between the TA approach for entrepreneurship education and the predominant approach in UK HEIs: two such examples are students directing their own curricula, and the creation of a real business. In order to reconcile some of these differences, it is worth examining the learning and entrepreneurial theories providing a base from which UK HEIs might develop an equivalent approach to academic practice and learning.

Heutagogy

From a pedagogic perspective, TA is aligned with heutagogy (Hase and Kenyon, 2000). The term heutagogy is derived from Greek for self and leading (*agogos*), (Hase and Kenyon, 2007; McAuliffe et al., 2009). Heutagogy is defined as an approach to learning and teaching where:

[Learners] are highly autonomous and self-determined and emphasis is placed on development of learner capacity and capability with the goal of producing learners who are well-prepared for the complexities of today's workplace (Blaschke, 2012, p.1).

To place heutagogy in relation to other education theories – pedagogy and andragogy – we can consider the PAH continuum (figure 1) developed by Garnett and O'Beirne (2013):

	Pedagogy	**Andragogy**	**Heutagogy**
Locus of control	Teacher	Teacher/ learner	Learner
Education sector	School	Adult	Research
Cognition level	Cognition	Meta-cognition	Epistemic cognition
Knowledge production context	Subject understanding	Process negotiation	Context shaping

Figure 1: PAH Continuum, Garnett and O'Beirne (2013, p.139).

According to Garnett and O'Beirne (2013) there are distinctions between the educational theories, with the core aspect of heutagogy being that the learner is self-determined (also Blaschke, 2012). To further distinguish heutagogy from andragogy, which also emphasises SDL and is common in UK HEIs, central to the heutagogic learning (teaching) approach is development of the *learner* and the *process of learning*.

It is worth noting at this point the heutagogic view of learning and education. Hase and Kenyon (2003) argue that imparting and teaching knowledge and skills does not necessarily equate to actual learning. To the authors, rather than the teacher having control over the learning of an individual, it is only the learner who can learn (ibid). Thus, lecturers in HEIs would be the holders of knowledge and skills that are shared with students. The heutagogic learning process could therefore be defined as "an integrative experience where a change in behaviour, knowledge, or understanding is incorporated into the person's existing repertoire of behaviour and schema (values, attitudes and beliefs)," (Hase and Kenyon, 2007, p.112). Thus, from a heutagogic perspective, the purpose of learning is not only to build knowledge and skills as transmitted by pedagogy, but for an individual to be able to develop capabilities and competencies, defined as applying the underpinning knowledge and skill in a variety of unknown and changing contexts and situations. This is where heutagogic theory fits with the TA approach: the application of theory to practice in uncertain contexts.

The core aspect of heutagogy – the capability and competency to replicate learning in any environment – fits with the principal of what QAA (2012) would recommend for the delivery of entrepreneurship education in the United Kingdom. They state:

> [it is] important to provide readiness for a rapidly changing economy, and to enable individuals to manage workplace uncertainty and flexible working patterns and careers. Enterprising skills such as team working and the ability to demonstrate initiative and original thought, alongside self-discipline in starting tasks and completing them to deadline, are essential attributes that have been identified by employers as priority issues (QAA, 2012, p.4).

Heutagogy is also premised on the basis of double-loop learning and self-reflection (Argyris and Schon, 1996, cited in Hase and Kenyon, 2000). In double-loop learning, learners consider two aspects: first, the problem, with its resulting action and outcomes; and second, reflections upon the problem-solving process and how it influences the learner's own beliefs and future actions. Consequently, questioning one's own values and assumptions is central to how a person learns, and how they are able to do so in unfamiliar circumstances and contexts.

Furthermore, the purpose is not simply to understand how to solve a similar problem in a similar way in future, but instead to take on board the complex learning from that activity and embed it within the capability and competence of the individual. As McAuliffe et al. (2009, p.3) report, by pursuing a heutagogic approach, learners:

> learn continuously in real time by interacting with their environment, can learn through their lifespan, can be led to ideas rather than be force-fed the wisdom of others, can enhance their creativity, and thereby re-learn how to learn.

As noted, the ability to reflect is essential to the heutagogic learning process. This aspect is embedded across the TA approach and is found in many of the TA micro-cultures worldwide (it is strongly encouraged and indeed assessed in the UK versions of TA). According to heutagogic thinkers and practitioners (for example, Canning and Callan, 2010; Blaschke, 2012), the ability to be reflective is central to the learning process. Thus, in a heutagogic classroom, a learner is encouraged to be aware of new knowledge developed as a result of different ways of knowing, rather than relying on the pedagogic approach of knowledge and skills dissemination (Canning and Callan, 2010). Based on the importance of reflection, it is possible for students to demonstrate the qualities of heutagogy, such that they are: self-aware; able to articulate feelings, experiences and ideas; engaged in sharing discussion with others; able to investigate appropriate academic sources in developing their own theories and knowledge; and confident in their study skills (Canning and Callan, 2010, p.80).

Finally, heutagogy has been applied in a variety of different learning contexts, for example: in nursing, engineering, and education professions, and as part of organisational learning. It can also be identified as the underpinning *learning* philosophy for TA. But how does this fit with theories of entrepreneurship education and application? Effectuation theory (Sarasvathy, 2001) may be a possible link.

Effectuation theory

Effectuation is a theory of the entrepreneurial process (Arend et al., 2015). The theory proposes that rather than entrepreneurs possessing perfect knowledge, they proceed with their business activities in an environment of uncertainty until such times as they have achieved a satisfactory artefact (or business) (Sarasvathy, 2001). The entrepreneur undertakes the process based on several aspects and decision points. They first assess their available means, such as who they are and what and who they know. In tandem, they consider whether loss on the route to the desired end artefact is affordable. Thereafter, the process is about building interactions and gaining commitments from and with partners and stakeholders toward achieving the end artefact. Overall, in the effectual business creation process, the individual (and partners) do not seek to control the future, but shape and make the future within a context of uncertainties.

This theory of entrepreneurial business creation behaviour chimes with heutagogy and is evident in several aspects of the TA methodology. For example, self-reflection and self-awareness is crucial to both the business and learner aspects of TA: *who am I* and *what* or *who do I know* are vital reflective processes in the early stages of engagement. Thereafter, the team (or partner/stakeholder) aspects emerge. Finally, rather than seeking to have a base of business knowledge and skills which may encourage a view of control in the business environment, TA learners are both learning and doing simultaneously.

To summarise, heutagogy offers an alternative approach to learning, moving beyond knowledge and skills to capabilities and competencies supported by self-awareness, self-reflection and lifelong learning. Effectuation theory also identifies the importance of self-awareness, partnership working, and creating a business in a context of uncertainty. Together, both of these theoretical frameworks merge in the application of the TA approach (see figure 2). Yet how does this approach to learning translate to a UK HEI environment and our student cohort? Which aspects can be embraced? What are the challenges? Suggested approaches, including some that extend beyond the entrepreneurship discipline, are explored in the following section.

	Heutagogy	Effectuation	Team Academy
Locus of control	Learner	Entrepreneur	Learner
Education sector	Research	Post-education	Higher education
Cognition level	Epistemic cognition	Epistemic cognition	Epistemic cognition
Knowledge production context	Context shaping	Context shaping	Context shaping

Figure 2: The relationships between heutagogy, effectuation and Team Academy.

Applying Team Academy in a HEI context

Particular attention is given here to the value of heutagogy as authors identify both benefits and limitations of a heutagogic approach to learning in general and for the HEI context in particular (McAuliffe et al., 2009; Tosey et al., 2013). For example, McAuliffe et al. (2009) identify several benefits. They suggest that by using a heutagogic approach, education can facilitate the ability to learn, thus developing competencies and capabilities (ibid). This is because in heutagogic assessment, accountability linked to performance is assessed instead of memorisation (Jones, 2016).

Heutagogy can also enhance individual and collective creativity, and is especially relevant in the context of applied and vocational education and training environments. In addition, there are several TA practical tools that could be of value to HEI learning and teaching toolkits, and which extend beyond entrepreneurship education; these are outlined opposite.

Heutagogic tools

Learner-defined learning contracts	Learner-defined learning contracts provide the opportunity to understand the individual student more fully. Further, it provides a framework from which to identify what will be learned, how it will be learned and the complementary assessments. This is a reflective tool for students to really engage in their learning and to commit to that learning.
Flexible curriculum	TA is based on a flexible curriculum. This enables individuals to drive their learning, to determine what their needs are, and establish how far they are going to pursue that area of interest. This approach should encourage self-determined learning and greater investment from students. The flexible curriculum is supported by learner-determined questions and discussion. All TA programmes have several team sessions on a weekly basis in which different aspects of their learning are discussed. This contributes to the students' ability to learn and make sense of course content. It also allows for individual and group reflection, building skills in presentation and contributing ideas.
Assessment approach	Flexible and negotiated assessment is one of the most challenging aspects (for UK HEIs) of the TA approach, yet it does have merit and can be applied in numerous ways beyond student-set assessments. For example, building on the learning contracts that the students have developed themselves, assessment outcomes can be tied to their learning contract (learning goals). This approach has been shown to improve motivation of students (Blaschke, 2012).
Reflective practice	In addition to tools, it is also possible to build in the importance of reflective practice. This can be facilitated through learning journals that document reflective learning. In many TA programmes, this is built into the course and oftentimes forms part of assessment. The importance of reflective learning can also be reinforced during assessments through peer-peer feedback and through group work. The importance of feedback from coaches and other team members is crucial.

Challenges of a heutagogic approach

Despite these benefits and the practical tools of heutagogy, the challenges of applying this learning approach in a UK HEI may be more complex. First, there are several operational aspects of the HEI, which may be inconsistent with heutagogy, such as the educational expectations of HEIs, risk-taking attitudes, credentialising practice-based learning, and forms of assessment.

Second, there are features of the student cohort and expectations which must also be considered. Each will be discussed in turn.

HEI context

McAuliffe et al. (2009) discuss the expectations of education within a HEI environment. They draw specific attention to the amount of time there is available to HEI staff to work with students, and to the kind of complex problem solving that can be achieved in the time available. The planning and preparation requirements of this style of learning and the additional pressures on HEI staff workload are also of concern. McAuliffe et al. (2009) identify the risk-taking attitude of HEIs where justifying trialling new educational methods is limited: this is often linked to "fear of failure and repercussions in student feedback" (ibid, p.1). Moreover, particularly in courses that have professional body accreditation (such as engineering), HEI programmes and modules are required to fit those external criteria. McAuliffe et al. (2009) also identify the significant challenge of assessing this kind of learning and its outcomes. Heutagogy, according to McAuliffe et al., is concerned with the "use-value" (ibid, p.4) of the learning. This is ultimately driven by the realities of the marketplace into which a student may enter (as may be identified by professional bodies), rather than based on HEI criteria of what it is meaningful to know. Further, in a heutagogic approach, assessment is democratised, whereby assessment content and inclusion is decided by students in line with marketplace requirements. From first-hand observation, this is the case in the Finnish programmes. Students have assessment goals to meet, but they are solely responsible for regulating whether they have achieved those or not.

Student cohort and expectations

In addition to the HEI operational context we must consider the students themselves: their desires and expectations of education and their educational history to date. McAuliffe et al. (2009) draws attention to the entire life-cycle of education. Given that most undergraduate students arrive at an HEI direct from school-style education, it could be considered foolish to expect them to embrace a learning approach such as heutagogy, which is essentially appropriate for adults. Furthermore, McAuliffe et al. (2009) reported findings from a student survey about learning styles, discovering that students' main concern was passing assessments to gain qualifications, rather than with the specific goal of learning. Thus, heutagogy as a learning approach does not necessarily reflect existing learning styles and the pragmatic approach to learning taken by many students: undoubtedly, a key limitation to the use of the heutagogic learning approach within HEI.

Heutagogy in context

Finally, in addition to specific learning-style benefits and limitations, we must also consider the applicability of the TA approach beyond its Finnish context. This aspect of TA has been the subject of research conducted by Tosey et al. (2013). The authors conclude that TA is *not* replicable and transferable beyond its original development in Jyväskylä, Finland. TA is context specific. Thus, the implementation of TA in other contexts will be subject to change and development in line with the local micro-culture. This is not surprising; nor does it represent an insurmountable challenge given that TA exists in several HEIs in countries beyond Finland. However, the key components of a TA approach (for example, the five philosophical values, business creation, team working) and how they may operate in a different micro-culture require attention.

To this end, based on their UK study, Tosey et al. (2013) identify four key attributes of a learning environment, which should be considered, and to which the TA approach can be adapted: social embeddedness, real-worldness, identity formation, and normative considerations. Social embeddedness refers to the importance placed on team working: how could this key collaborative aspect be included in existing courses? Perhaps a move beyond individual working toward self-determined team-based projects? Real-worldness emphasises the importance of real-world risk in a supportive environment. How much can an HEI enable students to come face-to-face with non-HEI consequences? As an example, when Finnish TA students make a mistake, they are subject to the real-world consequences such as being fired from business deals and losing business contracts. Identity formation is about the affiliation and membership that students who join a TA programme feel. How does language, process, activity, and communication reinforce the brand of the course or activity? Is there a coherent message in your course about its purpose and how does it stimulate buy-in from students to encourage participation? Finally, the normative aspects concern the underpinning ideology of the learning and teaching approach. It is necessary that one remains critical about the messages integrated in a course and reflects on the micro-culture established.

To summarise, heutagogic learning as expressed through the TA approach is innovative and demonstrates some impressive learning outcomes for the TEs. It also employs several tools which could be implemented in UK HEI entrepreneurial education programmes and other disciplines. Yet it is not without its challenges, especially its fit with UK HEI culture and academic quality frameworks.

Conclusion

According to recent QAA and other employer publications, business graduates are not fully equipped to enter the labour market. This may in part be due to the approach taken in HEIs for the delivery of entrepreneurship education. In seeking to explore alternatives to the gaps in the current approach, this chapter has considered Team Academy, an innovative approach for entrepreneurship education developed in Finland and now used worldwide. Key aspects of the approach include the importance of team work and responsibility, ownership, and control of (entrepreneurship) learning. Thereafter, the underpinning learning and entrepreneurship theories were examined. Heutagogy is the learning theory associated with TA, which prioritises self-determined learning, especially the development of competencies and capabilities for use in uncertain situations. Effectuation theory, an entrepreneurial process theory, fits with heutagogy and is specific to entrepreneurship. The examination of heutagogy and effectuation theories in the context of TA enables a richer understanding of the methodology, making a meaningful contribution to overcoming some of the existing challenges of UK HEI entrepreneurship education delivery. Furthermore, the importance of geographic context indicates that this approach to entrepreneurship education will be constantly evolving and responding to its micro-culture.

Finally, the chapter reviewed several instruments from the TA toolkit that could be implemented in HEIs for both entrepreneurship studies and beyond. By using some or all of these heutagogic learning principles and tools we can help to develop more world-ready graduates with a commitment to lifelong learning.

Implications for practice

Beyond application in the entrepreneurship education context, there are several implications for the practice of employing a heutagogic approach to learning. First, the importance of learner ownership cannot be underestimated. Consider relinquishing control and management of student learning and giving responsibility and ownership to the student. This could be facilitated through effective use of learning-contracts. Second, in concert with passing control of learning to the student, consider re-examining and potentially revising the learning philosophy of the classroom. Small steps such as planning assessments together with students at the beginning of the course may be one such option. Third, create a living curriculum, which is relevant to individual student interests and knowledge journeys. To control time commitments with regard to planning, passing management of this aspect to students will be in keeping with the heutagogic approach. Finally, supporting and developing a culture of self-reflection and honesty between students and lecturers/teachers. This requires a leap of faith and belief in the value of this kind of learning for students and for ourselves.

Isla Kapasi is an early career researcher in the field of entrepreneurship. Her research interests include: critical entrepreneurship studies, entrepreneurship education, leadership, innovation, and gender. Isla is currently developing a Team Entrepreneurship programme at Edinburgh Napier University. She has in-depth experience of working with undergraduates, postgraduates, and MBAs. Prior to developing her academic career, Isla was involved in the public, private, and third sectors. She has run several small businesses and is currently a mentor for high growth firms in Edinburgh in partnership with Edinburgh Chamber of Commerce.

References

Association of Business Schools, Quality Assurance Agency for Higher Education and Chartered Management Institute (2014). *Twenty-first-century Leaders: Building Practice into the Curriculum to Boost Employability* [Online]. Available: http://charteredabs.org/wp-content/uploads/2015/02/21st_century_leaders_june2014_-_final_report.pdf [Accessed 2 February 2016].

Arend, R. J., Sarooghi, H. and Burkemper, A. (2015). Effectuation as ineffectual? Applying the 3E theory-assessment framework to a proposed new theory of entrepreneurship. *Academy of Management Review*, 40 (4), 630–651.

Bhat, P. P., Rajashekar, B. and Kamath, U. (2007). Perspectives on self-directed learning – the importance of attitudes and skills. *Bioscience Education*, 10 (1), 1–3.

Bhoyrub, J., Hurley, J., Neilson, G. R., Ramsay, M. and Smith, M. (2010). Heutagogy: an alternative practice based learning approach. *Nurse Education in Practice*, 10 (6), 322–326.

Blaschke, L. M. (2012). Heutagogy and lifelong learning: a review of heutagogical practice and self-determined learning. *The International Review of Research in Open and Distributed Learning*, 13 (1), 56–71.

Bramhall, M., Radley, K. and Metcalf, J. (2008). *Users as Producers: Students Using Video to Develop Learner Autonomy* [Online]. Available: https://www.heacademy. ac.uk/resources/detail/subjects/engineering/EE2008Conference/p057-bramhall [Accessed 15 March 2016].

Canning, N. (2010). Playing with heutagogy: exploring strategies to empower mature learners in higher education. *Journal of Further and Higher Education*, 34 (1), 59–71.

Canning, N. and Callan, S. (2010). Heutagogy: spirals of reflection to empower learners in higher education. *Reflective Practice*, 11 (1), 71–82.

Dynan, L., Cate, T. and Rhee, K. (2008). The impact of learning structure on students' readiness for self-directed learning. *Journal of Education for Business*, 84 (2), 96–100.

Garnett, F. and O'Beirne, R. (2013). Putting heutagogy into learning. In: Hase, W. and Kenyon, C. (Eds.). *Self-Determined Learning*. London: Bloomsbury.

Hase, S. and Kenyon, C. (2000). From andragogy to heutagogy. *Ultibase Articles*, 5 (3), 1–10.

Hase, S. and Kenyon, C. (2003). Heutagogy and developing capable people and capable workplaces: strategies for dealing with complexity. *Graduate College of Management Papers*, 166.

Hase, S. and Kenyon, C. (2007). Heutagogy: a child of complexity theory. *Complicity: An International Journal of Complexity and Education,* 4 (1), 111–118.

Henry, C., Hill, F. and Leitch, C. (2005). Entrepreneurship education and training: can entrepreneurship be taught? Part 1. *Education and Training*, 47 (2), 98–111.

Hoppe, M. (2016) Policy and entrepreneurship education. *Small Business Economics*, 46 (1), 13–29.

Jones, C. (2016) Enterprise education: towards the development of the heutagogical learner. *All Ireland Journal of Teaching and Learning in Higher Education*, 8 (1), 2541–2556.

Jones, C., Matlay, H., Penaluna, K. and Penaluna, A. (2014). Claiming the future of enterprise education. *Education and Training*, 56 (8/9), 764–775.

Jossberger, H., Brand-Gruwel, S., Boshuizen, H. and Van de Wiel, M. (2010). The challenge of self-directed and self-regulated learning in vocational education: a theoretical analysis and synthesis of requirements. *Journal of Vocational Education and Training*, 62 (4), 415–440.

Knowles, M. S. (1975). *Self-directed Learning: A Guide for Learners and Teachers.* New York, NY: Association Press.

McAuliffe, M., Hargreaves, D., Winter, A. and Chadwick, G. (2009). Does pedagogy still rule? *Australasian Journal of Engineering Education*, 15 (1), 13–18.

Quality Assurance Agency (2012). *Enterprise and Entrepreneurship Education: Guidance for UK Higher Education Providers* [Online]. [Accessed 19 February 2016].

Roberson Jr, D. N. (2005). The potential of self-directed learning: practical implications for facilitators of older adults. *Activities, Adaptation and Aging*, 29 (3), 1–20.

Sarason, S. B. (1990). *The Predictable Failure of Educational Reform*, San Francisco, CA: Jossey-Bass.

Sarasvathy, S. D. (2001). Causation and effectuation: toward a theoretical shift from economic inevitability to entrepreneurial contingency. *The Academy of Management Review*, 26 (2), 243–263.

Scott, G. (2010) *Student Managed Learning: Whales, Dolphins and Sharks* [Online]. Available: https://www.heacademy.ac.uk/resources/detail/subjects/bioscience/differentiated-learning-self-directed [Accessed 15 March 2016].

Silén, C. and Uhlin, L. (2008). Self-directed learning – a learning issue for students and faculty! *Teaching in Higher Education*, 13 (4), 461–475.

Tosey, P., Dhaliwal, S. and Hassinen, J. (2013). The Finnish team academy model: implications for management education. *Management Learning*, 1–20.

Wehmeyer, M. L., Palmer, S. B., Agran, M., Mithaug, D. E. and Martin, J. E. (2000). Promoting causal agency: the self-determined learning model of instruction. *Exceptional Children*, 66 (4), 439–453.

Publish and be damned: exploring problem-based learning through the establishment of a university press

Avril Gray

ABSTRACT

Set within an award-winning postgraduate vocational programme, this chapter explores the establishment of a publishing imprint (in an academic setting) as a problem-based learning (PBL) initiative underpinned by pedagogy for employability.

Navigating students' personal development expectations alongside the group dynamics of an ambitious public enterprise within an academic context can test the most experienced of teachers, and this chapter considers what happens when, within a PBL environment, student enthusiasm, once ignited and nourished, becomes inflamed; when the problem is not how to stimulate students' engagement with learning, but instead how to manage it. The associated risks of group conflict, and how group dysfunction can be exacerbated when a classroom group project transforms into a tangible work for public consumption, are also assessed. The exemplar presented has been widely commended, and duplicated, as a prototype for the establishment of a university press.

Keywords: problem-based learning in publishing studies, student motivation, group conflict, employability, public engagement

Introduction

One morning in December 1824, a threatening letter arrived for the Duke of Wellington. "My Lord Duke," began the now famous attempt at blackmail (Longford, 1969).[1] Wellington was a field marshal, cabinet minister, national hero, husband, and father, whose dalliance with the notorious London courtesan Harriette Wilson was about to be publicly exposed in her memoirs. His audacious response? "Publish and be damned." And publish they did.

Whether Wellington's battle cry was borne out of bravado or incredulity, it has more than a little echo each and every time lecturers embark on the live publishing project that sits within the second trimester of this year-long postgraduate degree.

Publishing is an industry beset with risk, not least reputational, legal, and financial, and the situation becomes even more tenuous when the publication is itself used as a vehicle to develop publishing skills in postgraduate students determined to enter the profession. At its best, the finished product[2] can serve to showcase the talents of its creators; it can embolden a team, instil confidence in the individual, and provide tangible evidence of employability. Conversely, as with any live project, a host of unforeseen circumstances – not least an over-reliance on the actual production of a tangible product – can lead to a hothouse learning environment, fractious group work and even disillusionment.

This chapter argues that incorporating a problem-based learning (PBL) approach is an important design consideration for professional academic programmes, to prepare students for the challenges and opportunities of a dynamic and fast-paced industry. Underpinned by theoretical considerations, reinforced by insights gained from a review of the literature, and drawing on the experience gathered from running the programme for nine years, it tackles the main barriers to PBL, and presents new ways of viewing both conflict and motivation.

The challenges associated with PBL and assessment are not new, nor are they peculiar to vocational programmes such as the MSc under consideration. They do, however, pose particular questions when situated in a postgraduate programme (as opposed to an undergraduate one), where the expectations of students, coming from a diverse range of previous HE institutions, can be seen to increase in direct correlation to the timing of the PBL (how close it is to the end of the year-long taught programme, for example) and the impending pressure of securing employment in one of the most competitive of the creative industries.

Here we must make a distinction between employment as a measurable graduate outcome, and pedagogy for employability, which relates to the teaching and learning of a wide range of knowledge, skills, and attributes to support continued learning and career development. In accord with Yorke (2006) and Pegg et al. (2012) *employability* relates to the skills and ability of the graduate to function in a job; it makes no claim to employment rates, industry specific or otherwise.

The course into which this PBL initiative (the creation of a publishing imprint) was posited is vocational, and distinguished by its industry focus and the application of relevant professional skills. It will come as little surprise to learn that publishing is an industry requiring "continuous professional development to update skills" (Banou and Phillips, 2008, p.107). Neither will it startle to note that such "learning is best managed by enabling students to appreciate how the simultaneous and sequential publishing functions are coordinated" (Baverstock, 2010, p.38). One way to achieve both is to incorporate PBL – specifically, industry-articulated group work – into the curriculum. From the outset, it was established that "employability", as directly related to students' career aspirations, would be the key concern of the PBL; although it may be of interest, particularly to other vocational programmes, that relevant employment as a direct measurement of success has identifiably increased year on year in the context of this particular programme.

Research into the pedagogic value of project and group work is well documented, and the arguments supporting its value in terms of employability are also widely acknowledged. Less abundant is literature directly relating to the discipline of publishing, thus making it appropriate to refer to research conducted in other fields to provide insights. Adhering to the findings of Gewurtz et al. (2016) whose eight principles across 11 theories of teaching and learning "provide the foundation for curriculum design" (ibid, p.59) for PBL within a university-based education programme,[3] a new module was developed and situated in the second trimester of this postgraduate programme. Of course, research into work-based learning (WBL) also espouses the value of real-world scenarios, but though similarities to the workplace exist in this module (somewhat artificially imposed), PBL, not WBL, formed the pedagogical approach.

PBL is not new to higher education and there is comprehensive research to support the benefits to student learning. Although studies are not so concerned with teacher engagement – and this chapter highlights the potential for research in this area – there is sufficient evidence of its worth to students to allow recommendations for teachers and practitioners, acknowledging that the perceived risks associated with innovative teaching practices can prevent their adoption by even the most venerable and experienced of teachers.

The following sections provide an overview of the PBL approach, context, and rationale, including research into PBL, group work, and conflict management in higher education. In evaluating the impact, future developments are outlined and directions for future research suggested. In summary, this chapter proposes engagement as the incentive to break down barriers to PBL for students and lecturers alike.

Rationale and risk of introducing PBL on a postgraduate programme

Fisher et al. (2004) see what they term a *tension* between the "staid or insular qualities" (ibid, p.16) of the university and its dynamism; in posing questions relating to the learning environment, they ask whether the ideal should offer students a more worldly learning experience in preference to the "ivory tower removed from local parochialism" (ibid, p.17). It is not within the scope of this chapter to comment on the sector at large, but the question is of interest when considering a vocational programme and the issue of employability.

Most trimester-long projects take a considerable amount of staff time to manage, and so the decision to embed a live publishing, or PBL, project[4] within the postgraduate programme was implemented after detailed and robust research. Literature advocating the merits of PBL in the classroom was examined and, as this was limited in terms of this particular discipline, the net was cast wider to include research conducted in other academic areas. Publishing as a discipline is relatively young and, as Bläsi (2015) notes, utilises book history and literary studies – both hermeneutical – as its academic foundation, with business studies and sociology providing additional sustenance. Indeed, this chapter goes further, being informed by the pedagogic findings of medical and health professionals, where research into PBL in the classroom is more advanced.

In addition, the preparatory stages included primary research into current industry demands, with the creation of an advisory panel and implementation of measures for sustained evaluation. Face-to-face interviews with the principal industry bodies were supplemented with discussions with alumni and employers. In addition, consultation with, and input from, the programme's accrediting body played a critical role in the design of the module.[5] The establishment of a Publishing Liaison Panel (set up with the purpose of informing the module, and comprising 12 members from the industry, some with experience in academia) allowed for in-depth and detailed discussion of the learning criteria against industry parameters. Hence, in a quadrumvirate approach, the needs of student, employer, accreditor, and institution (including staff) were considered and evaluated.

Against this positive, supportive backdrop, it was ascertained early on that a barrier to success lay in fear of failure (publish… and be damned?). Wellington appears to have had no doubts when faced with the prospect of public scrutiny, even ridicule. In the case of staff involved in this module, the potential for catastrophe went far beyond the personal. The aim was to publish and publicly distribute the output from the PBL group project. How would students achieve their career aspirations if the profession viewed their first foray into the industry as amateurish? How would the programme's reputation as a Centre of Excellence fare if its publishing outputs were derided? If the work was found wanting and publication vetoed, what impact would that have on the current student experience or on future students' engagement?

Preparing for action: a planned and integrated approach

Alongside these questions, the answers to which required an interrogation of the very aims of the programme, the development of this PBL module forced a reconsideration of the entire learning architecture: from a review of the overall programme structure, to the securement of sustainable funding (to enable publication and ensure the expectations of future students could be met). Careful consideration was likewise paid to the learning environment, which went as far as equipping two dedicated classrooms: one to facilitate industry specific hardware and software, the other to replicate a professional boardroom, as one might find in the publishing workplace. While it is not this chapter's recommendation that every PBL project requires this level of investment, it is advised that such concern for the learning environment should constitute part of any PBL strategy.

The macro environment thus supported, similar attention was expended on other aspects of the module's scaffolding, and avenues for student co-authorship were identified. A number of strategies were employed to provide for a collaborative approach, where students were encouraged to make decisions regarding their learning on the module; such overhaul of the learning environment penetrated to a consideration of the timetable.

For example, it was identified that the various personal, work, and logistic commitments of postgraduate students are not always conducive to group-based PBL. The expectation that groups meet extensively outside of class can jar with students' individual priorities. Thus, the importance of giving groups class time has been acknowledged as deserving particular attention (McKendall, 2000). This also gives the lecturer a chance to observe team behaviours. Furthermore, both Feichtner and Davis (1984) and, more recently, Pfaff and Huddleston (2003) found that providing more class time for group projects resulted in increased motivation, which, as a key driver in establishing the PBL for this programme, was a persuasive factor. Thus, the PBL would need to have class time and, going one step further, the timetable was reimagined and consolidated so that project classes occurred on a full day each week, allowing students to better manage other commitments. This had the added benefit of providing a clear structure, and fostered the desired workplace resemblance. To encourage student initiative, a supportive rather than instructional environment was adopted, with lectures delivered on a separate day, thereby allowing the focus of the PBL project class to be operational, while also apportioning time for a reflective and considered response to practical learning against a theoretical framework.

Marshalling the troops: a collaborative approach

Before moving on to examine the actual PBL project, we should pause to consider how this exemplar had group learning at its core. Assisting students with group projects can be one of the most challenging aspects of teaching. Likewise, studies have found that students can also approach group work with a distinct lack of enthusiasm. However, the module has surpassed expectations in terms of student engagement, and has in fact presented the opposing problem of managing, and at times actually restraining, this engagement.

Mindful of the research – much of it advising caution when confronting PBL, let alone the further complication of group work and the particular challenges it presents (Borg et al., 2011; Hansen, 2006; Hammar Chiriac and Granström, 2012; Payne et al., 2005) – specific attention was paid to the project group's construction. The principles of project and human resource management informed the decision to allow groups to self-select, following research conducted by Hilton and Phillips (2010), which indicates that students respond better when allowed to choose their group. Borg et al. (2011) also provide further justification for this approach, stating that it can prevent conflict. Interestingly, and concurring with the work conducted by Hilton and Phillips (2010, p.29) who found that in their own study "the actual grades assigned to the group projects did not differ between group formation conditions", a longitudinal review of the annual assessment grades over the PBL projects' lifecycle shows that this finding holds true in the context of this programme, even though student-selected groups perceive they produce higher-quality work. Despite this, as student engagement was the key driver here, it informed the decision to allow students to self-select their group.

Students were then invited to collaborate in other aspects of their learning environment – induction sessions were provided in advance of the module's start date, where students were given the opportunity to select the day they were in class, the PBL project they would work on, the group they would join, and the exact roles they would undertake in a group setting. Thus, from the outset, each student was encouraged to be an active – and accountable – participant in their own learning; a partner in their curricular design.

Central to the goal of encouraging student engagement, this allowed students an element of control over their learning environment. The positive effect on engagement was immediate and long-lasting. In the end-of-trimester questionnaire, students advised future cohorts to "work in many different departments" and "try and undertake multiple roles during the project in order to maximise the educational benefit on offer".[6]

Rules of engagement

The PBL projects have been running since 2010. Every year each student group (there may be multiple groups per year) delivers at least one output. This can take the form of a print or digital book, or both. That students have been so intensely connected to the tangible output is evidenced annually anecdotally, at one-to-one feedback sessions, by means of the (anonymous) module questionnaire, and by the examples of passionate, even fiercely defensive and confrontational attitudes expressed during the process, as will be seen.

Set against other criteria, student engagement did not feature top on this module leader's list of reasons for having a group output (and a tangible one at that – a publication that would be publicly distributed). However, the decision proved to be significant and dramatically increased student motivation. Year on year, staff have observed a real cohesion within each group, as cohorts evidence their engagement with a consistently high attendance on the module (both in and outwith class, with some even working beyond the 13-week duration of the module). No negative impact on the goals that had been established at the outset was identified, and a longitudinal study carried out for internal purposes revealed that engagement actually appeared to have undergone an exponential increase as a direct result of the decision to create a tangible output.

One way of ensuring that the output (the publication) was achievable was to align it with SMART objectives (Doran et al., 1981), and it is notable how many of these have engagement at their core. The following list has been augmented and honed by successive groups' consideration of their goals.[7]

S – specific, significant, stretching
M – measurable, meaningful, motivational
A – agreed upon, attainable, achievable, acceptable, action-oriented
R – realistic, relevant, reasonable, rewarding, results-oriented
T – time-based, time-bound, timely, tangible, trackable

Regular review and evaluation points help to assess whether each PBL project is aligned to these SMART goals. Group meetings and presentations in class allow staff to formally appraise the PBL at each stage. Primarily and practically, these meetings enable staff to review the achievements of the group, monitor the contribution of individual members, and approve the project's direction. More importantly, perhaps, regular meetings foster a collaborative approach, where students receive support and feedback on ideas, and are directed by staff. Such support is available throughout the day, but this structured meeting also provides a forum where all individuals can voice ideas. To promote whole group co-operation, methods were implemented to encourage quieter students to contribute, and thus to develop confidence in public speaking. Students may not have been fully aware of this at the time, but comments gleaned after the completion of one PBL project reveal that this was acknowledged by at least some students:

> Don't be afraid to speak up… everyone needs to contribute.

T can stand for *time* or *tangible*, and the published work is able to fulfil the latter: time being one trimester. Within this clear timescale, a series of deadlines is enforced. In addition, the students are made aware that attainment of their objectives is dependent on the group's willingness and ability to extend the timescale if required. This provides clear demonstration of the students' engagement with the PBL project.

What was perhaps less identifiable in terms of engagement was the effect of the tangible output. When outlining the PBL project's overarching objectives, measurements of success – specifying exactly what would constitute fulfilment of group objectives (published product, completion of learning outcomes, or a combination of both) – were also identified. *A* can mean *agreed*: the students are asked to identify their individual and group objectives, which are informed by, but not limited to, the module's learning objectives. It is notable that with each successive cohort a tangible outcome has been consistently high amongst students' agreed list of priorities.

However, from the outset (at the module planning stage) staff identified that the tangible product would not be considered as a measurable or assessed outcome, there being too many unknowns outwith the control of the students. Again, this has proved to be a pivotal decision, delivering a critical impetus to increased student motivation and engagement. As students have seen the fruition of their work as being within their control, this task conflict (the question of publication) has been a unifying and motivating force.

Note that for this PBL approach, the module's learning outcomes may be distinct from the group's objectives, which are unique to each PBL project group and are formed by the students as co-authors of their learning environment, as evidenced by Bovill et al. (2011). That the outcome was tangible was identified early on as a key driver for student engagement. The creation of a physical object (including digital as well as print) has been a principal motivational factor for students, and this has presented the most challenging aspect of the PBL publishing project.

The transformative powers of peer pressure and conflict

Slavin (1984) is not alone in asserting that students are motivated by the desire to gain social approval and avoid social sanctions. Added to this, the PBL publishing project operates on the currency of future benefits (specific and vocational). Peer pressure has led to increased motivation, which has been demonstrated by student collaboration outside of the allocated classes. While peer pressure has been greatly debated and is generally viewed as a negative force, its effect in this module has been overwhelmingly positive. Interestingly, the group tends to come together as a more cohesive force when facing the challenges and adversity associated with any PBL.

Here we arrive at perhaps the most formidable aspect of this PBL module, as it is this aspect which, as a body of research shows, can create the greatest barrier – in students and lecturers alike – to embracing group-based PBL. Conflict.

Recent studies by Borg et al. (2011) examine how conflicts arise within group work in higher education, and how they are perceived and managed by teachers. Payne et al. (2005) conclude that students' main concern about group work appears to centre around the fear of group conflict.

Shedding light on why PBL is not universally adopted by lecturers on vocational programmes, Hitchcock and Anderson (1997) argue that students' poor interpersonal skills and previously-formed bad habits can lead to an over-reliance on lecturers (thus increasing an already high workload for staff, and raising concerns about the real value of PBL to student learning) or, perhaps more worryingly, can result in such groups actually becoming hostile towards the lecturer.

Taking an almost Wellingtonian stance, Langfred (1998) suggests that group cohesiveness is not a holy grail and that students – and teachers – should be willing to manage conflict and perhaps even welcome it. This is a difficult pill to swallow. Modern lecturers are beset on all sides, within the institution and without, and it seems counter-intuitive to invite conflict into the classroom. Before opening that particular door, a consideration of why conflict should be viewed as a productive force in learning will be helpful.

Most academics will accept that there are two kinds of potential conflict in any group activity – task conflict and interpersonal conflict. While the latter should be avoided, Parise and Rollag (2010) suggest that too little task conflict is actually a bad thing. Without enough disagreement or debate, teams may quickly settle on a strategy before a full evaluation of the associated risks or problems. The problem of too little task conflict can be seen in the phenomenon of *groupthink*. Whether led by a dominant team member or group preference of the easier, less controversial option, individuals are reluctant to challenge the group consensus. The lack of debate or discussion can ultimately damage a team's effectiveness. Of course, the reverse can also prove true, where too much task conflict can lead to endless debate and repetition of the same arguments, wasting time and eroding motivation and, in the worst cases, resulting in interpersonal conflict. Thus, fearing that any task conflict will escalate into interpersonal conflict, many teams try to avoid or ignore conflict. Such task-conflict avoidance, argue Parise and Rollag (ibid), is detrimental to effective group work.

Thus, "healthy" task conflict is to be encouraged in group PBL, and yet lecturers are not supported by research or training to help them address this complex issue. Understanding the various ways that individuals deal with conflict is the first step towards managing it in groups and, by promoting conflict, engagement may in fact be enhanced – an unexpected, but welcome, outcome of this publishing PBL project. As early as 1974, Thomas and Kilmann discovered that people vary in their response to conflict along two dimensions: *assertiveness* (the extent to which individuals attempt "to satisfy their own concerns") and *co-operativeness* (the extent to which they try to satisfy the concerns of other people) (Kilmann and Thomas, 1977, p.310). These two dimensions help define five conflict-handling styles: competing (assertive and not cooperative), collaborating, compromising (midpoint on both dimensions), accommodating, and avoiding (neither assertive nor cooperative). Further, they found that alongside a situational response, national culture can influence the style people adopt when dealing with conflict. This is notable in the context of this programme, since this MSc, similar to postgraduate programmes across the UK, is international in its approach and student profile. Hence, the very diversity that provides rich resources for problem-solving can also create conflict, as individual students fail to appreciate the different thinking styles of others in their group.

Again, it is useful to consider the findings of medical and health professionals who have used PBL in the classroom. Hitchcock and Anderson (1997, pp.19–24), for example, identified five different small group dysfunctions:

1. Apathy, or lack of meaningful interaction
2. Limited or focused discussion that ignores (or refuses to consider) other aspects of an issue

3. Dysfunctional group member, who does not participate or perform equally with others
4. Scapegoated student, who becomes ignored by other group members
5. Domineering, argumentative or disruptive student(s), who prevent(s) others from learning through the process

The pivotal role of group relationships in PBL led Skinner et al. (2012) to develop what they term "a profile of 'ideal' PBL group dynamics" and to investigate how students themselves interpret the actual dynamics of their group. Their research often revealed that, in practice, PBL groups diverge from this conceptual ideal. A significant difference was the value students placed on an enjoyable climate and fun in learning, "which is not part of our conceptually ideal group climate" (ibid, p.200). Notably, positive comments from students who completed the publishing module also highlighted this aspect of enjoyment:

> Enjoy yourself as much as possible and get involved with every aspect of the project – you will learn so much, it is a great module!

The study conducted by Skinner et al. (2012) also found that, for some students, the hallmark of a good group was "no disagreements". As previously discussed, task conflict is healthy, common, and necessary for team growth. Task-related disagreements within the group and, as this chapter hopes to convey, even with the lecturers themselves, is not to be avoided, but managed. Earlier research by Barrows (1988) concluded that learning to think and behave as novice professionals involved students learning to establish professional working relationships: "[Students] must learn to deal with interpersonal dynamics throughout their professional careers as they will inevitably have to work with people with whom they may not naturally get along well" (ibid, p.12). That students' conception of group relationships is not fully focused on the conceptual (or professional), may help to account for the negative interactions with other group members and with teachers, and explain why task conflict can mutate into interpersonal conflict.

Highly effective teams and, this chapter argues, lecturers acknowledge from the beginning that conflict is often inevitable. Groups agree to confront task conflict as a team and not allow it to become personal. Early research by Thomas and Kilmann (1974) led to the development of the Conflict Mode Instrument (TKI®), a tool reputed to deliver insight, empowerment, and resolution to anyone involved in conflict. Hitchcock and Anderson (1997) recommended three strategies for conflict management, and offered a model for strategic intervention. Their work has led to the commonly acknowledged six strategies for managing group conflict. These strategies are used individually or in combination to help each publishing student group reach an effective resolution, and it is notable how all focus on the concepts of understanding and communication:

1. Clarify expectations at the beginning of the project
2. Discuss conflict openly as it arises
3. Ask questions to appreciate the situation from other perspectives
4. Recognise that the emerging conflict may not be the real conflict
5. Generate multiple options for resolution
6. Use third parties to help mediate conflict

Covey (2013, p.5) adds to this, advising, "seek first to understand, then be understood". This is excellent advice for anyone facing emerging conflict in or with groups. Borg et al. also provide ideas for prevention and resolution of conflict in student groups (2011, p.12), and all have been useful at various times to staff leading this publishing PBL model.

The experience gained supports the theory that, like any good manager, the lecturer should not only welcome task conflict, but introduce it as a catalyst to explore new and creative problem-solving approaches. Encouraging students to investigate a wide variety of options helps create an open and flexible learning environment to assist group agreement (relying on peer pressure), if not consensus. However, the risk is that, confronted with such task conflict and unable to navigate the changes that it generates, some groups or individuals within groups may complain of a lack of structure or succumb to the phenomenon of groupthink. The result is transference of the argumentative, defensive, interpersonal conflict towards the lecturer as instigator of the task conflict.

Peer pressure is a daunting force, and is yet another barrier to lecturers' adoption of PBL. It does not simply refer to persuasion tactics, but can also include passive behaviour, such as students not undertaking an action for fear of peer social sanction (Bursztyn and Jensen, 2015).[8] As discussed, this may result in groupthink, and even in hostility towards lecturers, as identified by Hitchcock and Anderson (1997). However, while group or peer pressure can have negative impacts, akin to conflict, it can, conversely, also be a motivating force, as demonstrated by this publishing PBL project. The danger is that student engagement may mutate and intensify to such an extent that it exerts undue pressure on individual students to achieve unfeasible group results. The challenge for this programme has been to funnel the powerful and intensive student response to PBL into a positive force. Indeed, such is the high level of student engagement that staff frequently need to intervene and restrain peer pressure when it contributes to overly ambitious interpretation, and even unrealistic expansion of the PBL outcomes and SMART goals.

Not only should the PBL project be meaningful and relevant (McKendall, 2000), but it should also present a manageable workload for the teams (Feichtner and Davis, 1984; Pfaff and Huddleston, 2003) and the individuals therein. The latter can be especially difficult to achieve when staff confront an intensified student engagement and inflamed expectations. To reign in ideas and risk conflict with the group or individuals is, as has been discussed, an approach lecturers will naturally try to avoid. However, as has also been shown, conflict in itself may not, in the longer term, be detrimental to student learning, and may in fact serve to strengthen and enhance student engagement.

Risk and motivation increase with public engagement

An increased challenge is faced when the project moves away from the classroom and out on to a new learning landscape. When, as is the case here, the PBL envisioned has public engagement at its core, staff as well as students need an injection of Wellington's courage as they prepare for external scrutiny. At the kernel of the ambition for this module was employability, and tied to this was the understanding of the benefits of working with external partners such as schools (as identified by the Research Councils UK). Thus, the idea grew to enhance the PBL's working-environment simulation with a project encouraging students to work with externals as collaborators in their learning journey.

It is important to take a little time here to detail the reach and impact of the PBL publishing imprint initiative in order to fully appreciate the increased risk of student engagement and the potential for disillusionment and complaint.

Advance, not retreat: opening the PBL project to public engagement

Taking one PBL publishing project as an example, fulfilment of the objectives involved consultation with schools, libraries, and reading organisations. This in turn evolved into a much more multifaceted and fluid approach, where students worked with stakeholders. In this example, primary school children, having been identified as the audience, were consulted at each stage of the production of a book that was targeted at them as readers. A city-wide marketing campaign involving a drawing competition captured the public imagination, and far surpassed expectations in terms of participation in that over 300 drawing completion entries were received. Eight libraries, four bookshops, and four primary schools were visited to gain in-depth market research. Over 200 primary school pupils[9] aged between seven and eleven years old were asked about their reading habits, and invited to provide opinions and feedback on a selection of book covers that the PBL group had created. As the project developed, it became clear that it had connected with a very real public concern about the decline in children's reading, and particularly that of boys.[10] That the project linked directly with staff research in this area is a motivational concept to which we will return, providing as it does another incentive to lecturers considering PBL.

Public engagement took various forms, from virtual (social media activity on a number of platforms, including Facebook, Twitter, and blogs) to terrestrial (including events and liaison with public and private bodies). Linkages were established on a local, national, and global level.

A motivating force for students and staff

With the potential amplified, so the risk intensifies. An increased number of stakeholders, a hothouse learning environment – where highly motivated students navigate a learning precipice – and a project that skirts conflict and faces public scrutiny, can create a highly charged atmosphere, one from which lecturers may justifiably flee.

However, to engage does not always have to mean wage war, as the experience from six years of managing this PBL model demonstrates. When student teams embrace PBL challenges in a positive way, and conflict is avoided, the benefits can include increased motivation for staff. The same can be said for public engagement. Fisher et al.'s (2004) idea of a more worldly learning environment provides a touchstone for this PBL's overarching objectives, including that of motivation. Likewise, Ostrander (2004) proposes a civic-engagement perspective that calls for students (and staff) to consider issues and questions that have a resonance for the communities they seek to reach. Thus "true partnership" has at its essence the research question.

This is evident in this particular PBL project: not only does it raise its own particular and internal questions, it often serves to augment a larger research question. When considering the rationale behind PBL in the classroom and tackling the issue of staff motivation, the concept of research may help not only to bolster student engagement, but also to provide lecturers with the fighting spirit to vanquish fears relating to group work. Admittedly, the value of the PBL to research was not part of the rationale identified at the outset of this publishing model, but it has formed a key component of PBL going forward.

Conclusion: reflections on impact

An overview of the consolidated impact of the PBL module in this postgraduate programme can be distilled into two main areas: programme and individual.

The success of this programme's particular PBL model can be evidenced by its adoption in other UK institutions (the template having been exported via two research students) and the attention it has received from international academics who have visited the University to research the model offered here. The PBL initiative has been cited as a key contributor to the programme's success in gaining accreditation, making it the only such programme in the UK to achieve this accolade.[11] At a sector level, the PBL project has, in effect, resulted in the launch of a University "press" or imprint, and the publicity surrounding this has resulted in an identifiable increase in the number of UK institutional imprints, imitating the one established here. Even more publicly, the project has rekindled the debate surrounding the institution's role and control over information dissemination on the international stage.

However, it is perhaps at the individual level that the most surprising and positive results have been demonstrated. The inter-relationships established in the group, and the connections made with external stakeholders, have generated a richly collaborative learning environment. This in turn has had an affirmative effect on both staff and students, with the latter encouraging peers to be more ambitious in their engagement and – interestingly unprompted – acknowledging the importance of overcoming fear to fully engage with group-based PBL:

> Get involved with everything you want to do. Don't be afraid to take on a lot and learn new things too!

Learners cannot be self-directed or life-long learners without strong metacognitive skills, which Dunlap (2005, p.7) refers to as "taking conscious control of learning". The publishing PBL project provides students with the ability to direct their own learning, and to establish group objectives within a clear framework of SMART goals and module learning outcomes. In addition, the students' comments indicate a positive experience, which Dunlap proposes will increase their self-efficacy. Self-efficacy theory suggests that this experience can have long-term positive impact on students' future effort and persistence, and instil the confidence to engage in challenging activities, perhaps even to encourage engagement in life-long learning, an ability and attitude which is seen as essential to employers.

The issue of employability has been cited as a key driver for the PBL approach, and this has been true for the students as well as for the staff who conceived the module. While the tangible product can have a benefit at interview level, thereby fulfilling the employability goal, "employability" cannot be measured by job success. However, students who successfully completed the module have been provided with concrete and demonstrable skills, and, by way of the peer and self-reflective elements of the assessment, encouraged to a deeper self-awareness within the PBL environment (Boud et al., 2001).

Public engagement is not the concern of this paper, except as a contextual barometer of student expectation. However, its impact is measurable and research is being conducted as to the ways in which the current publishing PBL project could embed a public engagement element, regardless of the specific project, and how this activity can be evaluated according to pre-defined metrics. In addition, the motivational impetus of research linkages cannot be overlooked: experience from this PBL example demonstrates how PBL projects can both inform, and be informed by, student and staff-directed research. This mutually stimulating collaborative approach can also help lecturers overcome barriers to introducing PBL in the classroom.

To date, this publishing imprint has published and distributed thousands of books; reached hundreds of children and young adults in schools, libraries, prisons, and hospitals across Scotland; and worked with countless partners. The ambition is only limited by the students' imagination, and by the extent to which lecturers can restrain their enthusiasm in line with the specific objectives, while exemplifying professional standards.

This is a crucial point on which to end: the result of engaging students as co-authors of their learning, and creators of their PBL goals, has been an intensification of motivation. That the product is both tangible and published has been held as a critical objective by students, a consequence that had not been fully appreciated at the outset. The question of how much this output should be staff-directed is much debated, particularly in terms of the students' (public and professional) accountability. Underpinning this was the decision to make a distinction between the measurement of assessment and the tangible product, and instead redirect the focus to the processes, procedures, and methods involved. This allowed the practical application to be viewed through a theoretical and reflective prism. It is a key finding that this very separation served to heighten students' engagement with the project, and proved to be one of the most innovative aspects of this challenging enterprise. An unexpected, but very welcome, effect has been the impact on staff motivation, an outcome that was not fully considered at the outset but which could provide a rich and fruitful avenue for further research.

Immediate research and discussions have revolved around the role of universities in the promotion of book-reading culture, knowledge creation, and dissemination. This is not new, but what is truly innovative is the adoption of new methods of communicating knowledge, and the idea that the process itself can be a collaboration between learners and teachers. The experience of this PBL demonstrates that this aspiration can be realised, and it is possible for the institution to have its own publishing facility.

University imprints and presses are not unique, but what is pioneering is that this publishing imprint – emulating the workplace and navigating the personal development and group dynamic of a public enterprise – is set within an academic context. It is a model that has been emulated by similar programmes, and it is hoped that the reflections provided here will inspire staff and students alike within other academic fields to embrace PBL with tangible outcomes. Arguably, that such outputs be made publicly available can be seen as the ultimate pedagogical aim.

Avril Gray MA (Hons), MPhil., is a Senior Teaching Fellow, Lecturer and Programme Leader of MSc Publishing at Edinburgh Napier University, the first Publishing programme in the UK to have secured accreditation. Avril also led the successful accreditation of Edinburgh Napier's MSc Magazine Publishing programme, achieving a status unparalleled in the discipline. She is Secretary of the Association for Publishing Education, whose members include every UK institution offering Publishing studies. She is an external examiner and Publishing degree validator, and is frequently asked to judge at national industry awards. Prior to her career in academia, Avril gained over 20 years' experience in the publishing industry, during which time she ran her own publishing company for more than ten years.

Notes

1. As quoted in *Wellington – The Years of the Sword* (1969) by Elizabeth Longford. This has commonly been recounted as a response made to Wilson herself. See also: http://www.independent.co.uk/voices/rear-window-when-wellington-said-publish-and-be-damned-the-field-marshal-and-the-scarlet-woman-1430412.html.

2. Throughout, the term *product* is applied to the physical outcome: in this case, the publication (which can take the form of a printed or electronic book).

3. Gewurtz, Coman, Dhillon, Jung, and Solomon's (2016) eight principles are: 1) adult learners are independent and self-directed; 2) adult learners are goal oriented and internally motivated; 3) learning is most effective when it is applicable to practice; 4) cognitive processes support learning; 5) learning is active and requires active engagement; 6) interaction between learners

supports learning; 7) activation of prior knowledge and experience supports learning; and 8) elaboration and reflection supports learning (ibid, p.61).

4. From this point forward, the word *project,* as indicating the public engagement aspect of this live PBL initiative, should be assumed.

5. The MSc programme was the first and only course of its kind to be accredited by, at the time, the only accrediting body in the UK: the Periodical Training Council (now the Professional Publishers Association). The MSc has since also secured Creative Skillset accreditation, and again it was the first course to gain this accolade from the UK industry skills body for the Creative Industries.

6. Comments gleaned from the anonymous student questionnaire, completed at the end of the module. Throughout this chapter quotations used are from those students whose permission was sought and secured to publish their comments to the benefit of future students and the module in general.

7. The acronym is unpacked in a more comprehensive way than in most other contexts where one adjective is commonly provided against each letter.

8. Where students take actions that deviate from what they privately consider to be the optimal action (what they would do if others would not observe their actions) in order to achieve social gains or avoid social costs.

9. The use of the arguably archaic term "pupil" is used to provide a distinction between the primary-school-age children who participated in this PBL project and the postgraduate students concerned.

10. "Boys also tended to read less often and think less positively about reading than girls did." National Literacy Trust Report, 2014, based on responses from 32,000 pupils at more than 130 schools in the UK.

11. The Periodical Training Council applauded this MSc as "standard bearer" for all other programmes in the UK.

References

Banou, C. and Phillips, A. (2008). The Greek publishing industry and professional development. *Publishing Research Quarterly*, 24 (2), 98–110.

Barrows, H. S. (1988). The tutorial process. *Springfield, IL*, Southern Illinois School of Medicine, 1–5.

Baverstock, A. (2010). Where will the next generation of publishers come from? *Scholarly Publishing*, 42 (1), 31–44.

Bläsi, C. (2015). Publishing studies: being part of a cultural practice plus x? *Libellarium*, 8 (1), 147–156.

Borg, M., Kembro, J., Notander, J. P., Petersson, C. and Ohlsson L. (2011). Conflict management in student groups – a teacher's perspective in higher education. *Högre Utbildning*, 1 (2), 111–124.

Boud, D., Cohen, R. and Sampson, J. (Eds.). (2001). *Peer Learning in Higher Education: Learning From and With Each Other*. London: Kogan Page.

Bovill, C., Cook-Sather, A. and Felten, P. (2011). Students as co-creators of teaching approaches, course design and curricula: implications for academic developers. *International Journal for Academic Development*, 16 (2), 133–145.

Bursztyn, L. and Jensen, R. (2015). How does peer pressure affect educational investments? *The Quarterly Journal of Economics* 130 (3), 1329–1367.

Covey, S. (2013). *The Seven Habits of Highly Effective People*. Simon and Schuster.

Doran, G., Miller, A. and Cunningham, J. (1981). There's a S.M.A.R.T. way to write management's goals and objectives. *Management Review*, 70 (11), 35.

Dunlap, J. C. (2005). Changes in students' use of lifelong learning skills during a problem-based learning project. *Performance Improvement Quarterly*, 18 (1), 5–33.

Feichtner, S. B. and Davis, E. A. (1984). Why some groups fail: a survey of students' experiences with learning groups. *Organizational Behavior Teaching Review*, 9 (4), 75–88.

Fisher, R., Fabricant, M. and Simmons, L. (2004). Understanding contemporary university-community connections. *Journal of Community Practice*, 12 (3/4),13–34.

Gewurtz, R., Coman, L., Dhillon, S., Jung, B. and Solomon, P. (2016). Problem-based learning and theories of teaching and learning in health professional education. *Journal of Perspectives in Applied Academic Practice* [Online]. Available at: http://jpaap.napier.ac.uk/index.php/JPAAP/article/view/194 [Accessed 11 Feb 2016], 59–70.

Hammar Chiriac, E. and Granström, K. (2012). Teachers' leadership and students' experience of group work. *Teachers and Teaching*, 18 (3), 345–363.

Hansen, R. S. (2006). Benefits and problems with student teams: suggestions for improving team projects. *Journal of Education for Business*, 82 (1), 11–19.

Hilton, S. and Phillips, F. (2010). Instructor-assigned and student-selected groups: a view from inside. *Issues in Accounting Education*, 25 (1), 15–33.

Hitchcock, M. A. and Anderson, A. S. (1997). Dealing with dysfunctional tutorial groups. *Teaching and Learning in Medicine*, 9 (1), 19–24.

Kilmann, R. H. and Thomas, K. W. (1977). Developing a forced-choice measure of conflict-handling behavior: The 'Mode' Instrument. *Educational and Psychological Measurement*, 37 (2), 309–325.

Langfred, C. W. (1998). Is group cohesiveness a double-edged sword? An investigation of the effects of cohesiveness on performance. *Small Group Research*, 29 (1), 124–143.

Longford, E. (1969). *Wellington – The Years of the Sword*. HarperCollins Publishers Ltd.

McKendall, M. (2000). Teaching groups to become teams. *Journal of Education for Business*, 75 (5), 277–282.

Ostrander, S. A. (2004). Democracy, civic participation and the university: a comparative study of civic engagement on five campuses. *Nonprofit and Voluntary Sector Quarterly*, 33 (1), 74–93.

Parise, S. and Rollag, K. (2010). Emergent network structure and initial group performance: the moderating role of pre-existing relationships. *Journal of Organizational Behavior*, 31 (6), 877–897.

Payne, B., Sumter, M. and Monk-Turner, E. (2005). Conflict resolution and group work. *Academic Exchange Quarterly*, 9 (2), 22–6.

Pegg, A., Waldock, J., Hendy-Isaac, S. and Lawton, R. (2012). Pedagogy for employability. *Higher Education Academy* [Online]. Available at: https://www.heacademy.ac.uk/sites/default/files/pedagogy_for_employability_update_2012.pdf [Accessed 6 Feb 2016].

Pfaff, E. and Huddleston, P. (2003). Does it matter if I hate teamwork? What impacts student attitudes toward teamwork. *Journal of Marketing Education*, 25 (1), 37–45.

Research Councils UK [Online]. Available at: http://www.rcuk.ac.uk/pe/partnershipsinitiative [Accessed 10 Feb 2016].

Skinner, V., Braunack-Mayer, A. and Winning, T. (2012). Getting on with each other: PBL group dynamics and function in problem-based learning. In Bridges, S., McGrath, C. and Whitehill, T. L. (Eds.). *Clinical Education: The Next Generation*. Springer, 189–205.

Slavin, R. E. (1984). Students motivating students to excel: co-operative incentives, co-operative tasks and student achievement. *The Elementary School Journal*, 85 (1), 53–63.

Thomas, K. W. and Kilmann, R. H. (1974). *Thomas-Kilmann Conflict Mode Instrument*. Mountain View, CA: Xicom, a subsidiary of CPP Inc., 1–16.

Yorke, M. (2006). Employability in higher education: what it is and what it is not. *Learning and Employability*, Series 1. York: ESECT/Higher Education Academy [Online]. Available at: http://www.heacademy.ac.uk/assets/documents/employability/id116_employability_in_higher_education_336.pdf [Accessed 6 Feb 2016].

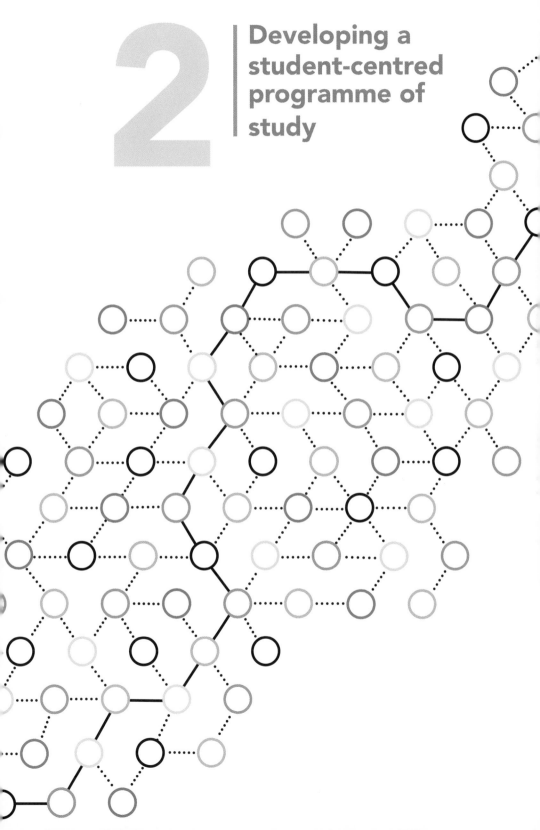

2 | Developing a student-centred programme of study

Developing a reflective and empirically-informed undergraduate research methods module, including a worked exemplar

Jennifer Murray

ABSTRACT

Teaching research methods is challenging for both staff and students. Adequate skills acquisition in the area of research methodology and data analysis is important across disciplines, as students undertaking an honours project or seeking postgraduate study are expected to be capable in these areas in order to achieve their degrees. Across Higher Education Institutions (HEIs), research-informed teaching is becoming a target and indeed providing a gold standard in teaching practice. As such, it is important that the design of research methods modules is aligned with this practice and empirically informed. The aims of this chapter are to present a method of redesigning undergraduate research methods modules informed by pedagogic and subject-specific literature, illustrated by a worked example of a third-year undergraduate psychology research methods module as an exemplar of the process. While the key focus is on redesigning a module, the pedagogic and empirical literature and many of the steps outlined in the exemplar can be applied to the design of any new module. Reflection on the process of redesigning the exemplar module and engaging with the literature is presented, which complements the key aim of the chapter: that is, to present a structure for the pedagogically and empirically informed redesign of a research methods module. To conclude, a high level of engagement with research methods can be achieved with careful consideration of what we should and should not use when teaching undergraduates about research methods and analyses.

Keywords: research methods, redesigning research methods modules, empirically informed module design

Introduction

> It is very easy to assess computational aspects of statistics and it can be left to others to examine the extent to which this is an essential part of the learning process. Assessing statistical thinking, however, is a much more challenging activity (Hewson, 2014, p.6).

This statement demonstrates one of the key issues often considered by those who teach research methods and statistics to undergraduate students. We must adequately balance the so-called easy assessment of the procedural aspects of carrying out data analyses with the need for assessing students' interpretative abilities, whilst also fostering an environment in which students can develop their understanding of research methods.

The overarching aim of this chapter is to present a method for redesigning undergraduate research methods modules, supported by pedagogic literature and subject-specific empirical literature. Additional reflection on the process of redesign will be presented to complement the more evidence-based focus, providing a fuller view of the process of module redesign. While the key focus is on *redesigning* a module, the pedagogic and empirical literature and many of the steps outlined in the exemplar can largely be applied to the initial design of a module as well. This chapter will therefore summarise the literature around designing and delivering effective, empirically-based undergraduate research methods modules (including qualitative and quantitative analysis needs). It will discuss the use of active learning tasks and reflective learning on students' improved understandings and capabilities in this subject area, aiming towards deeper learning. It will then provide a reflective account and a worked exemplar of a suggested design and delivery method, discussing the redesign of an undergraduate third-year psychology research methods module. Hence, it will share both an empirical summation and a true example to encourage best practice and consideration for module design in this area.

Context and rationale for this pedagogic project

Teaching and learning research methods, data analyses, and their interpretation is challenging for both staff and students (Hewson, 2014). There are a number of factors that can accumulate to increase these challenges, but none which are insurmountable, as this chapter hopes to demonstrate. Before discussing methods to improve teaching and learning in research methods, identifying why this matters must be considered. Gaining the appropriate research skills is required at universities across most, if not all, disciplines.

In their final year, students are largely required to undertake an independent honours project as a major component of their degree. Being equipped with the methods and analytical skills is therefore absolutely required for the completion of this project and to achieve the best degree classification within their abilities. In addition, students seeking postgraduate study are expected to be capable in these areas whilst some graduate roles require direct research skills or critical analysis as well as transferable problem solving skills, all of which are learned through conducting research and interpreting findings. Finally, across Higher Education Institutions (HEIs), research-informed teaching is becoming increasingly important in teaching practice. As such, it is important that the design of research methods modules is aligned with this practice and that these are themselves empirically informed. With increasing expectations to teach a wider breadth of material, the balance and maintenance of sufficient depth can be difficult to achieve.

The current project emerged from the need to redesign a third-year research methods module which had not been running as successfully as would be desired in terms of student and staff experience. Taking the above considerations into account, the process of a pedagogically- and empirically-informed module redesign was embarked upon, with module leadership having been taken over by the author. The module aimed to teach the students about research methods, to advance their quantitative, statistical analysis skills, and to teach them the theory and practice of complex qualitative analysis. In the first year, the module was run with only very minor changes, to identify where the module was successful and where it needed improvement. Monitoring the module and students in a tacit way each week, and through multiple module feedback evaluation questionnaires, the module leader identified a number of issues that had to be addressed before an optimal learning environment could be achieved. These issues related mainly to the module structure and assessment load. Specifically, the module review identified: a disjointed approach between the teaching of quantitative and qualitative aspects of the module; an excessive assessment load; a greater focus on process and quantitative methods over holistic research approaches, qualitative approaches, and interpretation; and a general lack of methods/research skills being taught. It was therefore clear that the module had to be redesigned to better suit students' needs and encourage better quality teaching, learning, and assessment strategies.

Description of activity

In order to ensure that the redesigned module would be properly informed by and designed within a pedagogic and subject-specific empirical context, a review of teaching and module design literature was conducted. This was followed by a review of the existing structure of the module, and a subsequent redesign of the structure and content of the module, in order to balance and equalise student perceptions about the importance of the module's key components (research methods, quantitative approaches, and qualitative approaches). Each of these three key tasks will be presented and discussed below.

Review of teaching and module design literature

Considerations when designing modules

> Modules are not developed in isolation, but within a course or programme structure, and the process is informed by the external national qualifications framework and, where relevant, professional body requirements (Donnelly and Fitzmaurice 2005, p.101).

To contextualise the need for the consideration of wider literature when designing or redesigning modules, higher education academic literature will be discussed in addition to a review of recent developments in the wider Scottish educational context. The context of the exemplar module within its current programmatic structure, with its quality and assessment guidelines also being considered.

A major change in the way that education is delivered in Scotland for those aged 3–18 years was introduced in 2010–11 through the Curriculum for Excellence (CfE). The CfE has been labelled as a "progressive evolution" in the delivery of education in Scotland (Muir, 2013, p.10). The CfE was introduced to provide a flexible, coherent, and enriched curriculum (Education Scotland, 2013). It is centred on four key capacities, aiming for students to become successful learners, confident individuals, effective contributors, and responsible citizens (ibid). It ultimately aims to motivate students to become lifelong learners (ibid). The first cohort of CfE students to enrol in higher education will occur in 2016. It is prudent for HEIs to begin preparation early in order to best support students' transitions to university. One way of achieving this is to develop modules that have shared values with the CfE.

Murray (2015) argued that HEIs ought to share the values of the four CfE key capacities to smooth student transitions and experiences between school and higher education. In a similar vein, work by Bishop (2015), which investigated the disparity between student expectations of a course and their experiences, found that an incongruent experience led to lower student satisfaction and poor student retention. Logically, this disjointed perception-experience may also impact on student engagement with a course of study and hence subsequent learning. Within research methods modules, such as the exemplar, three of the four key CfE competencies can be embedded with relatively minor adjustments: "successful learners", "confident individuals", and "effective contributors" (Education Scotland, 2013). The capacity "responsible citizens" (ibid) in the wider context, is less applicable to research methods teaching. However, as research training and research ethics should be discussed within research methods modules to some degree, this capacity would be applied too.

Considerations within the teaching literature

To help students become successful learners, techniques encouraging active learning should be used. Active learning is an educational technique that aims to engage students, placing some of the responsibility for learning on the students themselves (Bonwell and Ellison, 1991). This is achieved by tasking students with both "doing things" and "thinking about the things that they are doing" (ibid). Academic and pedagogic literature has recognised the strength of active learning in improving student experiences and outcomes for over two decades (Yoder and Hochevar, 2005) as well as its association with promoting deeper learning and understanding (Qin, Johnson and Johnson, 1995). However the *sage on the stage* approach to delivering research methods teaching in Higher Education remains prominent. While this may be appropriate in some instances (for example, in delivering complex theory relating to qualitative approaches), statistical lectures can risk being dry and daunting for students. This is true of any abstract topic such as statistics.

Within the statistics teaching literature, a number of approaches are suggested to make abstract statistical constructs more concrete and to better engage the students in order to promote deeper, active learning. Within psychological literature, and increasingly other, related literatures (for example, applied health research/health literacy/health education), it is recognised that abstract concepts can be more difficult to interpret than concrete ones, which may affect learning (Rich and Chalfen, 1999; Williams et al., 2012). These concepts may consequently be less well-retained in memory than concrete ones (Walker and Hulme, 1999). Concrete words and concepts are those easily visualisable (for example: *dog, the dog ran,* or *there are four more apples on the table than there are pears*). On the other hand, abstract concepts and terms tend to relate to emotions, moods, or concepts that are challenging and difficult to visualise (for example, *wary, conscientious,* or *the logistic regression was run using variables X, Y, and Z, constraining the model to...*) (Paivio, Yuille and Madigan, 1968). This additional difficulty in interpretation associated with abstract concepts, such as statistics, may lead to an increased cognitive load, decreased optimal learning and impeded encoding of information for learning (Murray and Thomson, 2011). Within the teaching and learning approach for research methods modules, it is therefore beneficial to try to include more concrete examples and tasks when teaching statistics to aid understanding, conceptualisation (Rich and Chalfen, 1999; Williams et al., 2012), and retention in memory (Walker and Hulme, 1999).

To achieve this, two changes were made to the exemplar module. First, and most simply, the length of time spent lecturing on statistics was halved. This reduced the *sage on the stage* approach and the tendency towards surface-level learning. It also decreased the amount of time students spent listening to new and abstract concepts. In place of the decreased lecture time, additional tutorial time was added to allow students to discuss and explore the abstract concepts inherent in statistical research, with the aim of encouraging deeper learning. A second, more notable, change in approach was the inclusion of practical, student-inclusive tasks in the lectures, using accessible concrete examples when possible. For instance, the use of simple examples such as the number of cookies eaten by students in exam weeks compared to non-exam weeks allows statistics to be relatable and non-threatening.

This latter approach is supported by empirical recommendations proposed by De Maio (2013). An excellent example of an inclusive practical demonstration in a statistics context is proposed by Baker (2013), who suggested a simple, elegant, and highly concrete method to teach tests of differences in statistics. Using Baker's example, students would be provided with cookies in class and asked to count the number of chocolate chips in their cookie. A class data sheet would be created and the data analysed in class. This simple task could be modified to aid teaching in a number of statistical tests of difference; it is also easily adaptable, has a tactile aspect (counting the chips), and a reward (eating the cookie afterwards) that would encourage interest in the topic. Similar practical tasks could easily be integrated into the statistical lectures (albeit not necessarily always with cookies) to add a level of interest and intrigue each week. Schwartz (2013) used the candy M&M's in a similar way to teach statistics, and found that this technique was successful in encouraging student participation in class and in increasing the opportunity for active learning.

Combined with the intention to adopt concrete, easy to understand, and practical examples within the statistical lectures, the above suggestions are also in line with the recommendations of Doehler, Taylor and Smith (2013). They conducted a university-wide staff-student survey to identify ways in which students may feel better prepared to learn about and use statistics within the research requirements of their degree. These recommendations include using discipline-specific, relevant examples that make use of appropriate technology (if necessary) and have relevance to other modules.

Through increasing active participation in lectures, workshops and the introduction of tutorials within the exemplar module, the remaining two key drivers from the CfE are also addressed: effective contributors and confident individuals. Finally, to increase confidence and effectiveness of student contributions, the coursework for the statistical aspect of the module was altered; it developed from a test, workshop exercises, and a research report to a single portfolio, encompassing group and individual tasks. This involved students producing formal written work, a personal reflection, a group based task output, and in-class presentations. These will be discussed in greater detail later.

Reviewing an existing module structure and contextualising the need for redesign

Before embarking upon the redesign of a module, the existing structure and content should be considered in relation to other precursory and follow-on modules. How does it fit with other modules? What is the existing scope of the current module and does that fit with the entire programme of modules on offer? Are the structure and content within the module balanced? These can be deceptively difficult questions to answer, especially with busy academic years involving marking, planning, and so on.

It is tempting to make small changes on instinct, which is often without consequence. However, too many of these small changes can cause the design and subsequent delivery of a module to stray from a pedagogically sound base, and worse, leaves no room for incorporating the most up-to-date pedagogic evidence to the module design/redesign. There are also competing demands relating to academic ego. While change for the sake of change is never the best way, consulting up-to-date evidence and identifying what an existing module structure and balance looks like before making changes is a logical step to take.

This section will describe the original exemplar module structure, an undergraduate psychology research methods module. This will provide a vicarious learning opportunity and worked example of how this step was tackled in the redesign process, which could be used as a template in other similar research methods modules. To provide background context, the broad scope and history of the module will first briefly be presented.

Exemplar: original module structure

The exemplar module was a compulsory module for all third-year psychology students. It followed on from a second-year quantitative research methods module and fed forward into the fourth-year Honours dissertation project. The module aimed to teach students appropriate research methods and methods of analysis used commonly in psychological research to prepare them for their Honours projects and to provide the skills needed to critically evaluate published psychological research. It covered quantitative research, but was almost entirely focused on the process of statistical analysis; it also covered qualitative research, but, again, was almost completely focused on the techniques behind one analysis approach. These two areas were taught separately in their own silos and did not cross or correspond with each other within the module. The teaching staff taught on either the quantitative or the qualitative topics within the module, not both, hence appearing to students to be working independently of one another. This created a sense of disconnect among the students and a feeling that the module was almost made up of two mini-modules combined. To promote a more integrated learning opportunity for students, this discordance had to be addressed. The overall scope of the original module structure is shown in figure 1.

A second key issue was the content structure itself. While the module is described as a research methods module, it was biased in terms of time, content, and assessment towards statistical analysis. The actual research methods content within the module was restricted to four one-hour tutorials at the end of the trimester. The statistical component of the module ran throughout the trimester, with students receiving 37 hours of contact time on this and three coursework assessments. The qualitative component only ran for half of the trimester, with students receiving 18 hours of contact time and one assessment for this component. This led to students either cramming the statistical component and qualitative component into half trimesters instead of spacing out their study over the whole trimester, or to them viewing the qualitative component as a kind of addition of less importance, subsequently leading to poor performance on this component of the module.

This obvious imbalance in both content and perception had to be addressed in order to aid the depth of student learning on the topic of research methods, to equalise student perceptions of the three elements of the module (research methods, qualitative approaches, and quantitative methods), and to improve overall student performance and experience. A final concern lay with the volume and type of assessment that was employed on the module: two 2,500-word research reports, ten workshop exercises, and a multiple-choice test; it appeared excessive and was weighted to statistical processes (the *how to* rather than the *so what?*).

	Quantitative research (statistics)			Qualitative research		Research methods
	Lecture (2 hour)	Workshop (1 hour)	Tutorial (1 hour)	Lecture (2 hour)	Tutorial (1 hour)	Tutorial (1 hour)
Week 1	✗	✗	✗	✓	✗	✗
Week 2	✓	✗	✗	✓	✓	✗
Week 3	✓	✓	✗	✓	✓	✗
Week 4	✓	✓	✗	✓	✓	✗
Week 5	✓	✓	✗	✓	✓	✗
Week 6	✓	✓	✗	✓	✓	✗
Week 7	✓	✓	✗	✗	✓	✗
Week 8	✓	✓	✓	✗	✗	✗
Week 9	✓	✓	✗	✗	✗	✓
Week 10	✓	✓	✗	✗	✗	✓
Week 11	✓	✓	✗	✗	✗	✓
Week 12	✓	✓	✗	✗	✗	✓
Total hours	37			18		4
Assessments (% worth of module)	2,500 word research portfolio including a report (30%); 40 item multiple choice test (30%); 10 in-class workshop exercises (10%)			2,500 word research report (30%)		✗

Figure 1: Original structure for the exemplar research methods module.

Discussion of outcomes

To address the disparity between the volume and structure of the three components within the exemplar module, the three components were rebranded as workstreams: Workstream 1 (Qualitative Research), Workstream 2 (Quantitative Research), and Workstream 3 (Research Methods). While this is a very minor change, having all three components clearly labelled affirms that all three are of equal importance to the module as a whole, which should re-align students' perceptions of the importance of each workstream. In addition, the number of assessments for the quantitative and qualitative workstreams were equalised, with learning outcomes for research methods being embedded in both assessments. This again emphasised the equal importance of the three workstreams within the module to students.

The level of assessment on the module also needed to be readdressed, as it was excessive. Two of the assessments (the multiple choice test and the workshop exercises) promoted only surface-level learning (Higher Education Academy, 2011a), and students could pass these easily through pragmatic, superficial study methods, thereby not truly achieving the learning outcomes or aims of the module. Indeed, Brown and Knight (1994) reinforce the importance of assessment for learning. Thus, in order to align to good practice, redundant assessments ought to be removed or replaced.

To reduce the assessment load suitably and to promote deeper, active learning approaches (Higher Education Academy, 2011a) to the assessment, the assessment related to the workshops was removed from the redesigned exemplar, as was the multiple choice test. In its place, a portfolio format of assessment was introduced: one that could be replicated and applied to similar modules. These changes aimed to reduce the tendency towards surface learning and to encourage students to view the quantitative analyses as being linked to research and research methods, not just pressing buttons to analyse data and "get numbers off the computer". These changes are outlined in figure 2.

Within the exemplar's redesigned portfolio assessment, students design, plan, and write up a report on a quantitative research project, working in groups to mimic the real life research team experience.

Original workstream 2 coursework			Redesigned workstream 2 coursework		
Coursework component	% Module mark	Week due	Coursework component	% Module mark	Week due
2,500 word quantitative research report	30%	13	Quantitative research portfolio, consisting of: a) Project management plan for a research study; b) 1,500 word research report; c) Two in-class group presentations; d) 300 word reflection	60%	13, but presentations and project management plan would be worked on during class time and formative feedback would be provided in class
40 item multiple choice statistics test	30%	13			
10 in-class statistics workshop exercises	10%	13			

Figure 2: Original and redesigned exemplar module's quantitative workstream assessments.

To be able to successfully complete this group project, students must design and plan their research. This begins early in the module, within the research methods tutorials. This allows the students time and space to properly plan and gain experience of managing a research project, an ideal opportunity to prepare them for their fourth-year Honours project. Students develop a project plan and timeline, to be included in their portfolio. In class, they present their project plan mid-trimester, and again at the end of term; these are included as part of their portfolio. The latter presentation asks students to reflect on the changes required and challenges they faced within their project. This is to encourage reflection on the fluid and flexible nature of research and the skills that they may (or may not) have acquired through carrying out the project. These presentations give the students the opportunity to present their work and experiences in front of their peers and gain feedback, with the aim of assisting them in their understandings of their project for writing the report. They also provide a reflective summary of their experiences on the research, again allowing them to concretise their experiences into a learning opportunity.

An additional pedagogic approach that is of relevance and importance to the current module redesign is Constructive Alignment (Biggs, 1999). Constructive Alignment is "one of the most influential ideas in higher education" (HEA, 2011b). The introduction of Constructive Alignment in higher education teaching allowed lecturers to focus the design of their courses on intended learning outcomes. However, when this becomes procedure-based, there may be a risk of learning outcomes essentially becoming meaningless targets for which assessments are created and run purely as a means to an end. In the redesigned exemplar module, true alignment of learning outcomes, teaching, and assessment is employed. In Constructive Alignment, it is important to design teaching and learning activities in such a way as to meet learning outcomes, to have meaningful, actionable and achievable intended learning outcomes, and, finally, to design assessment methods in such a way as to truly assess and meet the intended learning outcomes. In the exemplar's redesign, the new teaching and learning approach and assessment better aligns with the intended learning outcomes: preparing students for and evidencing students' abilities in research design, process, and write-up.

Finally, in terms of contact hours across the three workstreams, clear bias towards the quantitative workstream was present, with approximately double the number of class hours being dedicated to statistics compared to qualitative methods, and only four hours being dedicated to research methods. The redesigned, balanced structure outlined in figure 3 aims to equalise the prominence of all three workstreams within the module, using appropriate teaching approaches (lectures, tutorials, workshops) for each topic.

Workstream 2 lectures were reduced to one hour to reduce the opportunity for passive learning approaches. This frees up time to extend the length of tutorials and workshops adopting a more active learning approach, making use of techniques such as the "flipped classroom", student-led presentations, and enquiry-based lessons. This is with the aim of encouraging deeper learning through the students being more active members of the learning environment, as well as linking in with the CfE's aims, as discussed previously.

	Workstream 2: quantitative research (statistics)		Workstream 1: qualitative research		Workstream 3: research methods
	Lecture (1 hour)	Workshop (2 hour)	Lecture (2 hour)	Tutorial (1 hour)	Tutorial (2 hour)
Week 1	✗	✗	✓	✗	✗
Week 2	✓	✗	✓	✓	✗
Week 3	✓	✓	✓	✓	✗
Week 4	✓	✗	✓	✓	✓
Week 5	✓	✓	✓	✓	✗
Week 6	✓	✗	✓	✓	✓
Week 7	✓	✓	✓	✓	✗
Week 8	✓	✗	✗	✓	✓
Week 9	✓	✓	✗	✗	✗
Week 10	✓	✗	✗	✗	✓
Week 11	✓	✓	✗	✗	✗
Week 12	✓	✗	✗	✗	✓ (1 hour)
Total hours	21		21		9
Assessments (% worth of module)	2,500 word portfolio (60%)		2,000 word research report (40%)		Assessed within other workstreams

Figure 3: Redesigned exemplar module structure.

Through adopting a student-led approach to workshops and tutorials, the students should become more confident in their understandings of the topic, and, with the addition of the formerly absent tutorials, will be given greater opportunity to discuss the topics that we cover in detail. This intends to encourage them to seek information independently for discussion, providing links once again to the CfE's key drivers. It is intended that students will be able to progress to Honours level with greater confidence in their research abilities, leaving them better prepared for their independent Honours project.

The extended length and decreased number of workshops allows students time in class to digest and discuss the statistical tests that they have run, and to hold discussions focused on interpretation, an area in which students struggle. This was a decision made with the aim of encouraging debate, discussion, and interpretation of what the students have learned, rather than students having to focus on "just getting through the tasks".

Future directions, recommendations, and conclusion

The evidence-based redesign of the module's workstream time allocations, along with the consultation of pedagogic and wider literature, goes some way to ensuring that the module is as effective in its teaching as possible.

This is not a feasible task at every module change time-point, given the plethora of other duties a lecturer must engage in. However, it is good practice to sit back and evaluate what the purpose of the module is – what it *should* be doing – and what it *is* doing. This is the first step towards thoroughly redeveloping a module. Following this, emphasis should be given to the relevant pedagogic and subject-specific updates to the literature, and to student and staff feedback. At this point, more major redesign can be carried out with confidence.

This chapter has summarised key, current literature relating to research methods module design and has provided a worked exemplar. The literature review served two purposes in this chapter. First, it directly informed the redesign of the exemplar module. In this sense, the learning and lessons presented within the literature review are easily transferable to similar types of modules across similar contexts. It would however be recommended that for modules which are not of the same subject or which sit within a different context, more subject- or context- specific literature should be consulted. The review's second function is to provide an example of good practice when redesigning, or indeed designing, a module. As discussed early in the chapter, teaching is expected to be underpinned by research within HEIs. Through reviewing both subject-specific empirical research, pedagogic literature, and local context education policy standards (such as the Curriculum for Excellence in Scotland), truly research-informed modules can be developed to promote best practice in teaching and learning.

While the exemplar is presented as an improvement within the undergraduate psychology programmatic structure in which it was based, it is by no means perfect, and indeed perhaps no module ever can be. It is hoped, however, that the reader will gain from this chapter the confidence to redesign their own research methods modules using the exemplar redesign process described, and that the literature review can provide a starting point for idea generation. The reader will be able to reflect on the research results presented, along with the worked exemplar and author's reflections on the process, allowing them to apply the lessons and suggestions to their own modules with confidence. Through collation of these lessons within this chapter, the process of redesigning modules using underpinning literature should also be swifter; an important aspect of working in modern HEIs. Finally, as with any module, the consistent monitoring of student feedback and performance in future iterations of the pedagogically-informed module will allow continued development and improvement.

Dr Murray is an expert in decision science and applies this expertise to research in the areas of forensic psychology and applied health research. Her pedagogic research has investigated modes of presentation for student memorisation, transitions across further and higher education, and statistics/research methods teaching. A Lecturer in Psychology at Edinburgh Napier University, she has taught research methods since 2007, and is passionate about engaging students in this difficult (and potentially bland!) area.

References

Baker, A. (2013). Teaching quality control with chocolate chip cookies. *Teaching Statistics: An International Journal for Teachers*, 36 (1), 2–6.

Biggs, J. (1999) *Teaching for Quality Learning at University*. Buckingham: SRHE and Open University Press.

Bishop, D. (2015). Aligning applicant expectations with student experience: a new approach to postgraduate recruitment and admissions processes. Paper presented at the Teaching Fellows Conference. Edinburgh Napier University, Edinburgh, 6 January 2016.

Bonwell, C. and Elison, J. (1991). *Active Learning: Creating Excitement in the Classroom AEHE–ERIC Higher Education Report no. 1*. Washington: Jossey-Bass.

Brown, S. and Knight, P. (1994). *Assessing Learners in Higher Education*. London: Kogan Page.

De Maio, F. (2013). Regression analysis and the sociological imagination. *Teaching Statistics: An International Journal for Teachers*, 36 (2), 52–57.

Doehler, K., Taylor, L., and Smith, J. (2013). A study of faulty views of statistics and student preparation beyond an introductory class. *Journal of Statistics Education*, 21 (1), 1–21.

Donnelly, R. and Fitzmaurice, M. (2005). Designing modules for learning. In S. Moore, G. O'Neill, and B. McMullin (Eds.). *Emerging Issues in the Practice of University Learning and Teaching.* Dublin: AISHE/HEA, 99–110.

Edinburgh Napier University (2012). Assessment handbook [Online]. Available at: http://staff.napier.ac.uk/services/vice-principal-academic/academic/LTA/Lists/Resources/Attachments/31/AssessmentHandbook_Dec_2014.pdf [Accessed 6 March 2015].

Edinburgh Napier University (2014). Edinburgh Napier University strategy 2020 [Online]. Available at: http://www.napier.ac.uk/about/management/DownloadLinks/Strategy_2020.pdf [Accessed 6 March 2015].

Education Scotland (2013). What is Curriculum for Excellence? [Online]. Available from: http://www.educationscotland.gov.uk/thecurriculum/whatiscurriculumforexcellence/index.asp [Accessed 1 August 2013].

Hewson, P. (2014) Editorial comment: Assessment. *Teaching Statistics*, 36 (1), 6.

Higher Education Academy (2011a). Deep and surface level approaches to learning [Online]. Available at: http://exchange.ac.uk/learning-and-teaching-theory-guide/deep-and-surface-approaches-learning.html [Accessed 6 March 2015].

Higher Education Academy (2011b). Constructive alignment – and why it is important to the learning process [Online]. Available at: http://exchange.ac.uk/learning-and-teaching-theory-guide/constructive-alignment.html [Accessed 7 March 2015].

Muir, K. (2013). CfE senior phase: raising your concerns. *The Scottish Education Journal*, 97 (2), 10–11.

Murray, J. (2015). Does the Curriculum for Excellence support students' aspirations, inspirations and motivations to attend university in the future? *Higher Education Academy STEM reports.*

Murray, J. and Thomson, M. E. (2011). Age-related differences on cognitive overload in an audio-visual memory task. *European Journal of Psychology of Education,* 26, 129–141.

Paivio, A., Yuille, J. C., and Madigan, S. A. (1968). Concreteness, imagery, and meaningfulness values for 925 nouns. *Journal of Experimental Psychology, Monograph Supplement*, 76 (1), 1–25.

Qin, Z., Johnson, D., and Johnson, R. (1995). Co-operative versus competitive efforts and problem solving. *Review of Educational Research*, 65 (2), 129.

Rich, M. and Chalfen, R. (1999). Showing and telling asthma: children teaching physicians with visual narrative. *Visual Sociology*, 14 (1), 51–71.

Schwartz, T. A. (2013). Teaching principles of one-way analysis of variance using M&M's candy. *Journal of Statistics Education*, 21 (1), 1–14.

Scottish Government (2013). Curriculum for Excellence – a quick guide [Online]. Available from: www.scotland.gov.uk/topics/education/schools/curriculum/ACE/cfeinaction/cfequickguide [Accessed 2 August 2013].

Walker, I. and Hulme, C. (1999). Concrete words are easier to recall than abstract words: evidence for a semantic contribution to short-term serial recall. *Journal of Experimental Psychology: Learning, Memory, and Cognition,* 25 (5), 1256–1271.

Williams, B., Anderson, A., Barton, K., and McGhee, J. (2012). Can theory be embedded in visual interventions to promote self-management? A proposed model and worked example. *International Journal of Nursing Studies,* 49 (12), 1598–1609.

Yoder, J. D. and Hochevar, C. M. (2005). Encouraging active learning can improve students' performance on examinations. *Teaching of Psychology*, 32 (2), 91–95.

Modelling pedagogic innovation in a Postgraduate Certificate in Learning and Teaching: risks and vulnerabilities

Julia Fotheringham and Kathryn James

ABSTRACT

This chapter explores the choices and decisions made during the redevelopment of a new Postgraduate Certificate in Learning and Teaching, aimed at new higher education academic staff. Drawing from two models of blended and online curriculum design, the chapter sets out the rationale for the innovative design that aimed to strike a balance between offering a manageable work-based learning experience for students while meeting the demands of internal agendas and external accreditations.

Core to its design is the programme philosophy to support an authentic learning experience for colleagues as students in the pedagogic discipline of learning and teaching. Focusing on this programme, which constitutes one 60-credit Master's level module, the chapter outlines the holistic approach taken toward redesign, delivery, and assessment. Well-established pedagogic tools such as learning contracts and patchwork texts are integrated with less familiar digital technology, and the advantages and challenges that this combination presents for participants is discussed. In recognising the unique position of new academic staff, the programme offers a logic for adopting technologies enabling flexibility of both learning route and assessment options to be woven into their own teaching and research practices.

Lastly, the chapter discusses the risks and vulnerabilities of innovative curriculum design for both staff and students. Staff face challenges when high levels of flexibility are offered, and students need to manage their decisions on a range of choices for both learning and assessment.

> Academics are all committed to keeping abreast of the latest research and ideas in their discipline, but few of them have the opportunity to keep at the forefront of developments in how to teach their subject (Dearing, 1997, p.31).

Keywords: e-portfolio, curriculum design, patchwork text

Introduction

The National Committee of Inquiry into Higher Education, more commonly referred to as the Dearing Report (1997), set requirements that all higher education institutions provide professional development in pedagogic practices for academic teachers. For most universities this resulted in the development of in-house Postgraduate Certificates in Learning and Teaching (PG Cert), centrally established and administered by the academic development team.

As a result of the many changes in higher education in recent decades, the implementation of recommendations from the Dearing Report (Clegg, 2009; Macfarlane, 2011; Gibney, 2013), the development of initiatives related to the UK Professional Standards Framework (UK accreditation framework for academic development courses) (Turner et al., 2013), and emerging discussions about the proposed Teaching Excellence Framework (Black, 2015; Hall, 2015; Williams, 2015), academic development units have two consistent and clear functions. First they should influence and encourage innovation and change in pedagogic practice based on scholarship, and secondly, they should provide staff development opportunities for academics (Hutchings and Shulman, 1999; Boud and Brew, 2013; Hibbert and Semler, 2015). Development of a revised PG Cert in Learning, Teaching, and Assessment Practice required not only the promotion of pedagogic innovation, but also the creation of a programme of professional learning that is aligned with the University's current strategic context and manageable in terms of workload for academic staff new to teaching.

This programme's redevelopment is of wide interest not only to academic developers who run their own Postgraduate Certificates (PG Certs) for new staff in higher education, but also for other academics who are faced with the challenge of redeveloping their own disciplinary curriculum in pursuit of innovation, academic rigour, and student satisfaction. Designers of professional work-based learning will recognise many of the challenges that this programme team encountered; particularly with regard to accommodating potentially divergent interests of students, managers, and academics of the discipline. This chapter outlines the key features of the redeveloped programme and explores the ways in which a balance was achieved between the need to meet the University's academic strategic priorities, the need to model pedagogic innovation, and the provision of an experience for students sufficiently flexible as to be responsive to their individual needs and disciplinary contexts.

Although the programme is still in its first year of implementation, the programme team have gained valuable experience of managing some of the risks accompanying pedagogic innovation, and of handling the vulnerabilities associated with new practices in learning, teaching, and assessment. A reflection on aspects of the development process that would be relevant to future progress is provided in the conclusion.

Redevelopment priorities

The new PG Cert Learning, Teaching, and Assessment Practice is a work-based qualification primarily intended for academics who are new to teaching in higher education. A priority for the programme team is to engage colleagues as students in authentic, practice-based academic development (Kreber, 2010; Loads and Campbell, 2015) that is guided by learning outcomes that connect both to their discipline and to the broader field of the scholarship of learning and teaching (Lindblom-Ylanne et al., 2006; Kreber, 2007). The programme team is mindful of potential students as newcomers into the academy and of their need to engage with new forms of knowledge that are located within policies, practices, and the rich traditions of their disciplines (Schulman, 2005; Trowler et al., 2012).

The perennial challenge for staff undertaking their PG Cert is lack of time, especially when many are fresh from the triumph and exhaustion of completing their PhDs. Furthermore, line managers keenly awaiting the arrival of new members of staff and looking forward to their making an early contribution to the work of the school or department are disappointed and frustrated if they perceive that their new colleague is unavailable for certain teaching or research activities because of their PG Cert commitments. For new staff, attempting to engage with a new role, a new place of work, and with 60 credits of Master's level compulsory study presents a significant challenge (Trowler and Bamber, 2005).

Creating a meaningful and manageable programme of professional learning that has potential to shape the way that students take on new forms of knowledge while also encouraging confidence and passion for innovative academic practice is no less of a challenge. The programme team are required to marshal their skills as change agents. Only then is it possible to lift the students' line of sight to look beyond the esoteric nature of the everyday, change their position, and turn their heads, supporting them to seek new horizons (Gadamer, 1975). As Webb notes "development, change, understanding and learning itself are all premised on a possibility of a movement of horizons" (1996, p.101).

Rationale for curriculum model

Fotheringham, Strickland, and Aitchison (2012) portray the higher education curriculum as a vehicle for the delivery of institutional agendas and priorities. The interest from managers and the University's leadership team in the redevelopment of the PG Cert Learning, Teaching, and Assessment Practice, offered evidence for this assertion. During that process of redesign, particularly when writing the programme's Aims and Learning Outcomes, the possibility of over-burdening this curriculum with competing priorities was recognised; for example, balancing attention on the development of skills and knowledge required for pedagogic research against the development of a repertoire of pedagogic strategies and tactics. The academic team faced difficult choices about the most appropriate content as it sought to progress institutional strategy in relation to learning, teaching, and external accreditor requirements, while also giving full value to the wide range of possibilities for pedagogic practice and promoting a deep engagement with the scholarship of learning and teaching. The team is in agreement with Fenwick (2001) when she critically examines the assumption that workplace learning is inevitably beneficial for workers. She notes that learning and its association with worker emancipation and independence is questionable where its chief driver is to ensure newcomers conform and shape themselves to the goals and strategies of the enterprise.

This sort of strategic action impacts on students required to participate in the programme in order successfully to negotiate probation. It also impacts on the programme team who are accountable to senior management for its design and successful delivery (Habermas, 1984; 1987). The same point can be made for other examples of professional work-based learning, especially where the programme is compulsory or linked to career progression and where the disciplinary or professional curriculum has to align with the exigencies of the workplace and the diverse needs of individual employees. Effective curriculum design cannot provide a solution for all of the complexities of workplace learning, but identifying a model of blended learning with potential to afford choice of modality of engagement, and personalisation of assessment, provided an excellent starting point for ameliorating the effects of any overwhelming adherence to institutional agendas, while at the same time giving due priority to the student's own disciplinary context.

Curriculum model: flexibility and choice

Devising the blend between face-to-face and online elements of a programme where students are distributed across a network of campuses and countries requires careful consideration. Many PG Cert students are unable to attend on-campus events given their portfolio of international and off-campus teaching responsibilities, while others are new to online learning, with the prospect of no face-to-face interaction for them presenting unwelcome challenges. Historically, the PG Cert programme had prioritised face-to-face delivery over online interaction, and there were expectations from line managers and new staff that this would be a continuing model. But it became very clear that given the resources available to the programme team for delivery and for the students participating in the programme, an online model with some face-to-face alternatives would provide a viable and flexible option. This could no longer be said for the previous traditional mode of delivery. The evidence in the literature is mixed when it comes to evaluating the learning gain and perceived value of online versus face-to-face learning which, given the complexity of the dimensions associated with the pedagogic inputs and student outcomes, is not surprising. However, there is sufficient evidence to suggest that where online (and blended) courses are designed to adopt pedagogically sound practices, they may provide equally effective and rewarding learning experiences (Driscoll et al., 2012; Ganesh et al., 2015). The choice of curriculum model was ultimately informed by a combination of research evidence, the team's expertise and sheer pragmatism – all of which will be a very familiar mix to many academics facing a redesign challenge.

Two different models of curriculum design informed the design of this programme: Staker and Horn's "flex model" (2012) and Carol Twigg's "buffet model" (NCAT, 2008).

Staker and Horn (2012) offer four models of blended learning in which each model configures a different balance between online, offline, teacher-led, and collaborative activities. The variation among these models signals the great diversity that exists in different blends, and an intention to choose blended learning as the mode of delivery is only the starting point of a series of careful decisions that need to be made by any design team. The flex model is the most relevant to this PG Cert development because it prioritises personalisation and choice in its description of a blend of learning whereby students move through a programme of study on an individual schedule of learning modalities. In practice on the PG Cert programme this means that each student has a degree of choice about which aspects of learning to undertake: online or face-to-face, individual or collaborative. Furthermore, students can undertake learning outcomes in the order that best suits their teaching and research practice and can attend corresponding workshops either face-to-face or online (synchronously or asynchronously) according to their preference and availability. Twigg's online buffet model (NCAT, 2008) also offers students individualised pathways, but through a programme of fully online learning. Importantly for the PG Cert, the buffet model deploys learning contracts as a tool to negotiate and agree on a personalised structure and direction through the programme.

In arriving at the final design, the team did not adhere exclusively to one or other strategy, but drew from lessons learned from delivery of the previous version of the programme, combining these with relevant features of blended curriculum reported in the literature. By applying established models of curriculum in the redesign process, the programme team are able to demonstrate an evidence-based approach to design and to reassure themselves and other stakeholders that although the design is innovative for a PG Cert programme, it is not without successful precedent, and is based on the best practice of other disciplines in different contexts. Being able to articulate such a design rationale for an untried approach has given confidence to reviewers during internal quality approval processes and to the programme's three external accreditors: the Higher Education Academy (HEA), the Nursing and Midwifery Council (NMC), and the Staff and Education Developers' Association (SEDA).

PG Cert programme design: an overview

The programme provides one calendar year of Master's level study. It comprises a single 60-credit module with nine learning outcomes organised into three thematic areas – *learning and teaching, assessment and feedback* and *pedagogic research and scholarship*. Each thematic area has its own section in the University's virtual learning environment, with resources for each learning outcome presented for online self-study in the form of an introductory text, multimedia resources, and introductions to relevant journal articles. Collaborative activity for each learning outcome takes the form of workshop activity and dialogue in online action learning sets (Currie et al., 2012).

Workshops are scheduled for online attendance mediated by WebEx, the University's online meeting and video conferencing tool, but face-to-face sessions are provided as alternatives. Students who are unable to attend either of these have the option to view the recorded online session and to join in with their peers in the action learning set which runs for the seven days following the workshops (Currie et al., 2012). Each student's choice of progression through the programme is negotiated, and a learning contract for each trimester is agreed with their personal development tutor.

Learning contracts serve a range of purposes for students and the programme team. Given the degree of choice available, there is a possibility for students to plan too much activity in one trimester, or to leave themselves with more required activity than could be reasonably achieved during the last few months of the calendar year. For the programme team, it would be hard to anticipate exactly how many students will be engaging with the thematic area that they lead, rendering workload difficult to forecast. These risks are alleviated by the deployment of a learning contract, a pedagogic device that has long been established in higher education (Knowles, 1975).

Students choose their learning outcomes from three thematic areas (see figure 1), and are encouraged to engage with learning outcomes that align with the types of activities reflected in their teaching timetables and other activities agreed with their line managers. This enables students to flex their engagement with the module in order to align their studies with their work commitments, and their personal aims and interests within each topic (Motschnig-Pitrik and Standl, 2012). This allows for adjustment to the demands of their workload rather than to a fixed curriculum or to the assessment calendar of the University.

No one feature of the programme design is particularly innovative in isolation, but it is the combination of tried and tested pedagogic techniques, the degree of choice, and the variety of modalities made available to students which together constitute an inventive approach to the design and delivery of this PG Cert in Learning, Teaching, and Assessment Practice. The assessment strategy provides a good example of an approach that has been documented in literature consistently (Winter, 2003; Ovens, 2003; Leigh et al., 2013), but the development of a patchwork text which spans the entire programme is unique in the context of PG Certs for new academic staff in the UK.

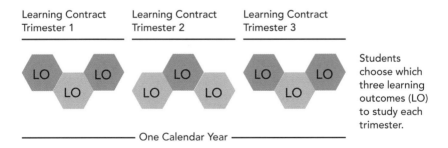

Figure 1: A learning contract outlining a plan to address
three learning outcomes is agreed each trimester.

Assessment strategy

The patchwork text is a feature of the curriculum design on the PG Cert that recognises the pivotal importance of assessment as a mechanism for shaping learning behaviours (Gibbs, 1999; Gibbs and Simpson, 2004) and the overall student experience on the programme (Medland, 2014). The strategy is consistent with an assessment for learning approach being one which prioritises a holistic programme experience, avoiding wherever possible the traditional and often constraining structures of academia (McKenzie, 2003). There are two key components to the assessment strategy on the programme: a learning contract and a patchwork text. The patchwork text comprises nine short critically reflective patches with supporting evidence and a wrap-around reflective piece drawing together learning from each of the separate patches developed over the year. The patchwork text is curated in Mahara, the University's e-portfolio, accessed from within the virtual learning environment.

Patchwork texts

A patchwork text consists of a collection of small complete sections built up over a period of time and brought together by a wrap-around text. Each patch provides a critical reflection on some aspect of teaching and assessment practice relating to one particular learning outcome. The written patch is substantiated by supporting evidence, which will vary according to the practice being explored in the patch, but which could include artefacts such as a relevant module descriptor, student evaluations or other feedback, an external examiner report, photographs, audio, or video. The nature of the supporting evidence will depend on the particular aspect of practice being explored in that patch and will be agreed in advance with a personal tutor and documented in the learning contract. In this PG Cert it is specified that each patch should not exceed 700 words, giving an approximate total of 6,300 words. This, together with an end of programme wrap-around text (2,500 words) that summarises the students' learning experience on the programme is submitted toward HEA Fellowship. This final piece of critically reflective wrap-around writing ensures that the completed patchwork text is not seen solely as an end point looking retrospectively at what has been learned, but also as looking forward to identifying areas for future development.

An important part of the induction to the PGCert programme includes an introduction to the patchwork text, and students are referred to articles in the literature which describe the rationale, benefits, and use of this type of assessment strategy in different disciplines. Details are provided in the programme documentation about how it will be used in the PGCert, and although the programme team have produced example patches because the programme is new, there are no completed patchwork texts to share with students. Furthermore, although the opportunity for personalisation and choice enables an appropriately customised work-based learning experience, it does limit the potential to show meaningful examples of what the students' own completed assessment outputs might look like. In subsequent years there will be complete patchwork texts together with wrap-around reflections available to share with new cohorts, but students in the first group are not so fortunate in this regard.

E-portfolios to support the assessment strategy

Portfolio assessments, such as patchwork texts and learning contracts, are not new and will be familiar to many students and teachers across all levels of education (Buckridge, 2008; Fitzpatrick and Spiller, 2010). In the PG Cert, the patchwork text is curated in an e-portfolio (in this case, Mahara) and the affordances for students sharing their work with each other enables connectedness and community: important aspects of the programme's learning, teaching, and assessment strategy. Mahara does not stand alone or outside the course. Rather, it is integrated holistically with the virtual learning environment and is designed to align constructively in coaction with the other learning technologies. The patchwork text word limit requires succinct and decisive writing, presenting a challenge even to the best writers. Students need to be selective with their choice of supporting evidence for the patchwork text's potential to be exploited. Without a connection to the patchwork text, evidence runs the risk of becoming a collection of documents and information, unconnected with and superfluous to the learning outcome being addressed. The e-portfolio supports this activity by providing the opportunity to present the connections and relationships between the texts and evidence in the same visual space while offering the functionality of linking to other mediums. This active process of reflection on the formal and informal, the gathering of evidence, its synthesis, and analysis all take a programme-focused approach that is holistic at its core (Laurillard, 1993; Thota and Whitfield, 2010).

Critiques of e-portfolio assessment strategies (Erikson et al., 2015) suggest that their format leads to fabrication, with students overstating their achievements and under-representing any deficiencies in their practice. However, the regular interactions between tutors, mentors, and students on this programme ensure that texts are not developed in isolation and the programme team remains confident in their assertions of their academic integrity. There are no doubt challenges; but, returning to the mantra of academic development, the programme team holds true to the ideal of creating opportunities and space for innovation, for risk taking and for collegial experimentation (Webb, 1996; Littlejohn, 2002; Clegg, 2009).

The introduction of any technology, particularly one such as Mahara that was unfamiliar to both staff and students, adds complexity to working relationships and heightens expectations, in addition to presenting unforeseen challenges. The e-portfolio creates opportunities for creative digital outputs and although the assessment strategy allows for participants to create multimedia artefacts as part of their supporting evidence, this does not mean that students have the interest or digital expertise required to do so. Successful innovation and technology adoption requires significant institutional support (Peacock et al., 2010) and the establishment of close working relationships with Information Services colleagues (Stockman and Truyen, 2011) with sufficient resource to provide expertise and support for tutors and students. Without the availability of this type of provision, students are unlikely to take advantage of the opportunities that the flexibility and format of the assessment strategy allows. Furthermore, tutors may feel vulnerable about their ability to provide leadership and support in relation to an innovative use of technology with which they are not yet fully competent or confident.

The risks of innovation

With any development that attempts to combine the traditional with the new, there are risks. For the students, the degree of flexibility and choice inherent in the programme's design requires strengths in time management, organisation, and self-motivation. As discussed above, new academics are busy familiarising themselves in a new environment and context, and competing priorities can overwhelm the best-intentioned student. Decisions made about the modality of engagement can be influenced more by availability than by positive choice or learning preference. Students who postpone attendance at face-to-face workshops and other forms of online engagement can potentially be left with no alternative but to engage with recorded seminars and out-of-date online discussions, which can lead to a sense of isolation from the cohort. Additionally, there is a risk that time pressures may lead to superficial engagement not only with the literature but also in participation in the wider programme activities. Cerych and Sabatier's (1986) classic study provides a timely reminder in this context that insufficient resources, including time to engage, can thwart expectations and hopes. Finally, in the commitment to promote and model innovation in pedagogic practice, there are ethical questions about the extent to which the innovative programme design constitutes added value to students' learning, or whether it places unnecessary hurdles for those who are unfamiliar with the format of study and the various technologies at a time when they have little capacity for further novelty, given their new surroundings and new work roles. The compulsory nature of the programme adds an extra layer of complexity to this ethical question.

Conclusion

This chapter has explored key features of the PGCert Learning, Teaching, and Assessment Practice and it has discussed aspects of curriculum redesign and pedagogic innovation pertinent beyond the context of this particular programme. In discussing the priorities for redevelopment it was suggested that competing agendas may encourage an overburdening of the curriculum unless a pragmatic view is taken of what might be possible given the constraints of the learning and teaching context. The conclusion drawn is that while it is not necessary to adhere strictly to any one model of curriculum design, an evidence-based rationale for a proposed innovation provides confidence to reviewers and external accreditors when considering the robustness of any proposed programme design untested in the discipline.

There is no single pedagogic feature in this development that is of itself novel. Instead, the innovation lies in the combination of the various elements of the programme and the technologies that are used to support their employment. Important ethical questions are raised about whether or not it is reasonable to expect students on a compulsory programme with no previous experience in many of the tools and techniques to engage with this degree of innovation, despite the potential added value to their professional development that the strategy brings. Accessible technical support has been identified as essential to support student engagement with the programme's various tools and processes and to fulfil the potential of this design. In the first year of its development, it is too soon to comment on whether the team have brought to bear an effective balance of tools, technologies, and technical support. A broad range of evaluative data will provide feedback on the design and create an agenda for future development. In the meantime, the programme team, who may be more familiar than the students with the design and different elements, continue to manage this strategically important programme and to cope with the vulnerabilities associated with its novelty.

Recommendations for developing workplace curriculum
- In order to avoid overburdening the curriculum, it is important to think holistically about the students' learning experience, to identify

overall priorities for the development, and to be highly selective about topics for inclusion and exclusion.

- When developing innovative curricula, a scholarly evidence base for the choice of curriculum design provides confidence for accreditors, stakeholders, and participants, providing a firm basis for the entire development.

- Pedagogic innovation can be achieved not only by implementing entirely novel approaches, but also by adopting established techniques and employing them in new disciplinary contexts supported in new ways by unfamiliar technologies.

- A patchwork text strategy provides valuable opportunities for personalising students' learning experience, accommodating the requirements for flexibility and choice in order to ensure meaningful assessment activity in workplace learning contexts.

- Sufficient, accessible technical support for staff and students is essential to the success of any innovation involving learning technologies.

- The risks to students' learning in any curriculum innovation need to be carefully considered and technical and pedagogic solutions sought to mitigate any such risks.

- Regular communication among a programme team is important given the feelings of vulnerability which is associated with developing curricula where tools and technologies are unfamiliar.

Julia Fotheringham is Programme Leader for the PG Cert Learning, Teaching and Assessment Practice which is a programme at Edinburgh Napier University for academics new to teaching in Higher Education. She also leads modules in the MSc Blended and Online Education. She enjoys working and learning with academics who are exploring ways of developing their practice in response to the changing environment of higher education. Her particular research interests are student transitions and professional learning.

Kathryn James has been an Academic Developer at Edinburgh Napier University since May 2014, having joined from University of Wales Trinity Saint David. While her role is to support academic colleagues with all aspects of their academic practice, she has a specific interest in learning technology adoption by academics and how this impacts and changes pedagogic practice.

References

Black, R. (2015). Higher Education Green Paper: have universities really neglected teaching? *Times Higher Education* [Online]. Available at: https://www.timeshighereducation.com/blog/higher-education-green-paper-have-universities-really-neglected-teaching [Accessed 4 April 2016].

Boud, D. and Brew, A. (2013). Reconceptualising academic work as professional practice: implications for academic development. *International Journal for Academic Development*, 18 (3), 208–221.

Buckridge, M. (2008). Teaching portfolios: their role in teaching and learning policy. *International Journal for Academic Development*, 13 (2), 117–127.

Cerych, L. and Sabatier, P. (1986). *Great Expectations and Mixed Performance*. London: Trentham.

Clegg, S. (2009). Forms of knowing and academic development practices. *Studies in Higher Education*, 34 (4), 404–416.

Currie, K., Biggam, J., Palmer, J., and Corcoran, T. (2012). Participants' engagement with and reactions to the use of on-line action learning sets to support advanced nursing role development. *Nurse Education Today*, 32 (3), 267–272.

Dearing (1997). *The Dearing Report, Higher Education in the Learning Society*. Main Report, London: Her Majesty's Stationery Office.

Driscoll, A., Jicha, K., Hunt, A., Tichavsky, L., and Thompson, G. (2012). Can online courses deliver in-class results? A comparison of student performance and satisfaction in an online versus a face-to-face introductory sociology course. *Teaching Sociology*, 40 (4), 312–331.

Erikson, M. G., Erlandson, P., and Erikson, M. (2015). Academic misconduct in teaching portfolios. *International Journal for Academic Development*, 20 (4), 345–354.

Facer, K. and Selwyn, N. (2013). *The Politics of Education and Technology*. London. Palgrave Macmillan.

Fotheringham, J., Strickland, K., and Aitchison, K. (2012). Developing and supporting the curriculum, *QAA Enhancement Themes Website* [Online]. Available at: http://www.enhancementthemes.ac.uk/docs/publications/curriculum-directions-decisions-and-debate.pdf [Accessed 4 April 2016].

Fenwick, T. J. (2001). Tides of change: new themes and questions in workplace learning. *Adult and Continuing Education*, 92, 3–17.

Fitzpatrick, M. A., and Spiller, D. (2010). The teaching portfolio: institutional imperative or teacher's personal journey? *Higher Education Research and Development*, 29, 167–178.

Gadamer, H. G. (1975). *Truth and Method.* 2nd ed. Translated by Joel Weinsheimer and Donald G. Marshall. New York: Crossroad.

Ganesh, G., Paswan, A., and Sun, Q. (2015). Are face-to-face classes more effective than online classes? An empirical examination. *Marketing Education Review*, 25 (2), 67–81.

Gibbs, G. (1999). Using assessment strategically to change the way students learn. In Brown, S. and Glasner, A. (Eds.). *Assessment Matters in Higher Education.* 41–54. Buckingham: Open University Press.

Gibbs, G. and Simpson, C. (2004). Conditions under which assessment supports students' learning. *Teaching and Learning in Higher Education*, 1 (1), 3–31.

Gibney, E. (2013). Robbins, 50 years later: experts discuss the development and legacy of the epochal report on its golden anniversary. *Times Higher Education* [Online]. Available at: https://www.timeshighereducation. co.uk/features/robbins-50-years-later/2008287.article?nopaging=1 [Accessed 2 June 2014].

Habermas, J. (1984). *The Theory of Communicative Action, Volume 1: Lifeworld and System: Reason and the Rationalization of Society*, Boston: Beacon Press.

Habermas, J. (1987). The idea of the university: learning processes. *New German Critique, Special Issue on the Critiques of the Enlightenment*, 41, 3–22.

Hall, R. (2015). Notes on saying "no" to the TEF [Online]. Available at: http://www.richard-hall.org/2015/09/16/notes-on-saying-no-to-the-tef/ [Accessed 30 March 2016].

Hibbert, P. and Semler, M. (2015). Faculty development in teaching and learning: the UK framework and current debates. *Innovations in Education and Teaching International*, March, 1–11.

Hutchings, P. and Shulman, L. (1999). The scholarship of teaching: new elaborations, new developments. *Change: The Magazine of Higher Learning*, 31 (5), 10–15.

Knowles, M. (1975). *Self-Directed Learning.* Chicago: Follet.

Kreber, C. (2007). What's it really all about? The scholarship of teaching and learning as an authentic practice. *International Journal for the Scholarship of Teaching and Learning*, 1 (1), Article 3 [Online]. Available at: http://digitalcommons.georgiasouthern.edu/ij-sotl/vol1/iss1/3 [Accessed 29 February 2016].

Kreber, C. (2010). Academics' teacher identities, authenticity and pedagogy. *Studies in Higher Education*, 35 (2), 171–194.

Laurillard, D. (1993). *Rethinking University Teaching: A Framework for the Effective Use of Educational Technology.* London: Routledge.

Laurillard, D. (2012). *Teaching as a Design Science: Building Pedagogical Patterns for Learning and Technology.* Oxon: Routledge.

Leigh, J. A., Rutherford, J., Wild, J., Cappleman, J., and Hynes, C. (2013). The patchwork text assessment – an integral component of constructive alignment curriculum methodology to support healthcare leadership development. *Journal of Education and Training Studies*, 1 (1), 139–150.

Lindblom-Ylänne, S., Trigwell, K., Nevgi, A., and Ashwin, P. (2006). How approaches to teaching are affected by discipline and teaching context. *Studies in Higher Education*, 31 (3), 285–298.

Littlejohn, A. (2002). Improving continuing professional development in the use of ICT. *Journal of Computer Assisted Learning*, 18 (2), 166–174.

Loads, D. and Campbell, F. (2015). Fresh thinking about academic development: authentic, transformative, disruptive? *International Journal for Academic Development*, 20 (4), 355–369.

Macfarlane, B. (2011). Prizes, pedagogic research and teaching professors: lowering the status of teaching and learning through bifurcation. *Teaching in Higher Education*, 16 (1), 127–130.

McKenzie, J. (2003). The student as an active agent in a disciplinary structure: introducing the Patchwork Text in teaching sociology. *Innovations in Education and Teaching International*, 40 (2), 52–160.

Medland, E. (2014). Assessment in higher education: drivers, barriers and directions for change in the UK. *Assessment and Evaluation in Higher Education*, (December), 1–16.

Motschnig-Pitrik, R., and Standl, B. (2012). Person-centered technology enhanced learning: dimensions of added value. *Computers in Human Behaviour*, 29 (2), 401–409.

National Centre for Academic Transformation (NCAT). (2008). *Six Models for Course Redesign* [Online]. Available at: http://www.thencat.org/R2R/R2R%20PDFs/Six%20Models%20for%20Course%20Redesign.pdf [Accessed 4 April 2016].

Ovens, P. (2003). A patchwork text approach to assessment in teacher education. *Teaching in Higher Education*, 8 (4), 545–562.

Peacock, S., Gordon, L., Murray, S., Morss, K., and Dunlop, G. (2010). Tutor response to implementing an ePortfolio to support learning and personal development in further and higher education institutions in Scotland. *British Journal of Educational Technology*, 41 (5), 827–851

Schulman, L. (2005). Signature pedagogies in the disciplines. *Daedalus*, 134 (3), 52–59.

Staker, H. and Horn, M. B. (2012). *Classifying K–12 Blended Learning.* Lexington: MA: Innosight Institute.

Stockman, C. and Truyen, F. (2011). *The Danger of the Downward Spiral: Teachers and Digital Literacy.* Proceedings of the 10th European Conference on e-Learning. Reading: Academic Publishing Ltd.

Thota, N. and Whitfield, R. (2010). Holistic approach to learning and teaching introductory object-oriented programming. *Computer Science Education,* 20 (2), 103–127.

Trowler, P. and Bamber, R. (2005) Compulsory Higher Education Teacher Training: Joined-up policies, institutional architectures and enhancement cultures. *International Journal for Academic Development,* 10 (2), 79–93.

Trowler, P., Saunders, M., and Bamber, V. (2012). *Tribes and Territories in the 21st Century: Rethinking the Significant of Disciplines in Higher Education.* Abingdon: Routledge.

Turner, N., Oliver, M., McKenna, C., Hughes, J., Smith, H., Deepwell, F., and Shrives, L. (2013). *Measuring the Impact of the UK Professional Standards Framework for Teaching and Supporting Learning (UKPSF).* Higher Education Academy [Online]. Available at: https://www.heacademy.ac.uk/sites/default/files/resources/ukpsf_impact_study_report.pdf [Accessed 4 April 2016].

Webb, G. (1996). *Understanding Staff Development.* Buckingham: Society for Research into Higher Education and the Open University Press.

Williams, J. (2015). Higher Education Green Paper: what it means for teaching. *Times Higher Education* [Online]. Available at: https://www.timeshighereducation.com/blog/higher-education-green-paper-what-it-means-teaching [Accessed 7 November 2015].

Winter, R. (2003). Contextualizing the patchwork text: addressing problems of coursework assessment in higher education. *Innovations in Education and Teaching International,* 40 (2), 112–122.

Reflections on students' experiences of practical group projects in media production education

Kirsten MacLeod

ABSTRACT

This chapter evaluates students' experiences of group work in media production education and investigates strategies for effective teaching and learning in that context. Working in groups can be challenging for students and for tutors supervising the logistics of practical production and assessment. Within the broader context of media education, media *production* education has lacked attention beyond debates over employability versus academic study. Strategies for teaching media production and students' experiences of learning through practical group work deserve further enquiry and discussion. This chapter examines theories of experiential education that have influenced strategies for effective group work, and considers in particular the management of group dynamics within a media production and learning environment. Furthermore, the chapter evaluates the outcomes of a survey of student learning experiences of group work, within the context of the literature relevant to media production pedagogy and to academic practice concerned with groups and practical work. It is concluded that carefully managed group work in media production education represents positive, iterative learning processes. A need for theoretical frameworks dedicated to questions of media production education is identified, together with areas for further research.

Keywords: group projects, media production, student experience, vocational training

Introduction

This chapter investigates methods of teaching and learning in media education focusing on the students' experiences of learning media production through practical group work. It examines issues relevant to group work and assessment within media production courses in Higher Education, and evaluates strategies for teaching and learning.

Higher education media production courses are characterised by the inclusion of practical group projects, where students work together as part of module assessments to produce short programmes, videos or films. This involves group work and practical activities, where students are reliant on each other in a process of collaboration by developing and drawing on each other's skills and knowledge. This approach to learning can be challenging both for the students working in these groups, and for the teachers supervising and managing the logistics of practical production and assessment within the academy. This chapter is relevant to media production pedagogy and more broadly to academic practice concerned with groups and practical work. It also addresses issues relating to employability and work-related learning in creative production education.

The research informing this chapter has employed a mixed methodology, combining a theoretical review of the broader contexts of media education and practical group-learning with a survey of student learning experiences in practical group work. Data collection and analyses are informed and contextualised by theories of education and group work considered in the literature review. Aggarwal and O'Brien (2008) and LaPrairie (2007) highlight relevant issues facing teaching and learning through project-based group work, which here are applied to a media education context. Dewey's theory of intelligent learning (1916) and Kolb's experiential learning (1984) frame Reynolds' (1994), Hanney's (2013), and Hanney and Savin-Baden's (2013) discussion and strategies for group production.

This chapter is intended to scope the potential for further research into group work in media-production education, and for raising the profile of the positive challenges of practical production work. The conclusions explore the limitations of scale of the survey sample and the value in testing the methodology.

Theoretical frameworks for group practice in media education

This review of literature surrounding teaching and learning in media education within the context of practical group work is multi-disciplinary, and covers research across studies of education, media, and management. The aim of this review is to highlight key theoretical themes in practice and pedagogy. These include the debates regarding vocationalism within media education, the skill-base of group practical production, group dynamics, and strategies for teaching and assessing.

Buckingham (2003, p.4) defines media education as "the process of learning and teaching about media," emphasising the knowledge and skills that learners acquire as its outcome. This process involves both reading and writing about media, developing "both critical understanding and active participation" (ibid, p.4), and enabling students to be both consumers and producers of media. Following Buckingham, this chapter recognises the term *media* as encompassing television, cinema, radio, video, photography, music, computer games, and the Internet.

The question of "what is media education for?" can be addressed by examining the dichotomy of the discourses of utility and employability versus theoretical study (Buckingham, 2003 and 2013; Berger and McDougall, 2013). Buckingham (2003) has railed against media education being repositioned and realigned with passing phases and with fads of education and political policy, such as new technology and creative economy. He traces the history of both practical and theoretical media-based education in the UK back to policies in the 1970s, which aligned education with vocation at a time when a rhetoric of skills and training dominated political influence on educational thinking. Berger and McDougall (2013) discuss how the worth of media education has traditionally been associated with its ability to deliver employability, "a media education is only any good if it is training people for the creative economy" (ibid, p.7).

Buckingham (2013) challenges the acceptance of vocationalism as conferring status on media education, suggesting that due to the forces of social inequality it does not necessarily translate into meaningful employment. Those who do succeed in media and creative industries are, he suggests, more likely to be "middle-class youth who pursue their digital enthusiasms in parallel with traditional forms of education leading to elite universities" (ibid, p.11), as opposed to those from more disadvantaged backgrounds studying media-based courses at universities that were once colleges or polytechnics. He argues that skills such as the ability to sell oneself and network, to be flexible, multi-skilled, and mobile, are the social capital which best equip the workers of present media industries (ibid, p.30).

Buckingham (2003) and Hanney (2013) both stress the importance of developing students' critical and creative abilities through the process of media education learning. This chapter is less concerned with the theoretical debate around the polarisation of practical skills versus written academic work, and rather focuses on approaches to learning that address practical group projects and production, acknowledging that they are a feature of media and film education across a spectrum of programmes with varying degrees of emphasis on employability and work-related learning.

Aggarwal and O'Brien (2008) draw on Ettington and Camp's (2002, p.357) definition of a group project as "a graded assignment requiring students to work collaboratively across multiple class periods and involving some time outside the normal class meeting." Project-based learning is broad and means different things in different disciplines and countries, and it involves a range of approaches, methodologies, and models (Hanney and Savin-Baden 2013, p.7). Its benefits include fostering high-level learning outcomes, and enhancing student learning by creating opportunities for critical thinking and peer evaluation (Aggarwal and O'Brien, 2008; Hanney, 2013; Hanney and Savin-Baden, 2013). Group learning is credited with promoting student learning and achievement, and with increasing student retention (Treisman, 1985; Wales and Sager, 1978). Aggarwal and O'Brien (2008) highlight how group projects offer opportunities for students to learn not just about the subject, but also about each other. Group project work fosters collaborative learning, which can enhance a student's sense of accomplishment and self-esteem, and provide more realistic learning experiences for students (ibid, p.2). For all the positive benefits, there are also drawbacks and dysfunctional aspects to group learning and group projects. These can develop from a range of issues, and are addressed further below in the work of Aggarwal and O'Brien (2008), Hanney (2013), and LaPrairie (2007).

As an integral aspect of project-based learning, group work and group learning must be critically addressed within a pedagogical frame. Approaches to group work have developed from educational pedagogies focusing on student-centred approaches to learning such as Dewey's (1916) intelligent learning and Kolb's (1984) theories of experiential learning. According to Reynolds, at the core of group work is an approach that "people can learn from each other as well as from teachers and that knowledge is constructed and reconstructed as a social process" (1994, p.26). Reynolds recognises that formal education should support this process and that, beyond time-based, output-oriented production projects, group work is also important for learning skills that can be applied to work contexts.

Kolb's (1984) theory of experiential learning is based both on the experience of events that have happened to an individual because of his or her own actions, and on the reflective observation of the consequences. This is seen through the lens of Kolb's learning cycle, which outlines a process of *doing, observation, reflection, conceptualisation* and *experimentation*, leading back to the concepts *doing* (or action) and *experience*. Kolb and Fry (1975) had previously argued that the learning cycle can begin at any one of the four points, and that it should really be approached as a continuous spiral.

With group project media education in mind, Reynolds (1994, p.32) applies Kolb's learning cycle into a "design for an activity" with similar stages of experience (group activity), observation and reflection (feedback of observations by trainers or participants), conceptualisation (discussion with or without instructors) and experimentation (planning for the future). Key to the relevance of Reynolds' scheme is the understanding that this is a model and should not be interpreted literally. As a model, it proposes an approach to group project (or group production) learning as a process. Reynolds also considers theories adapted from psychology, such as the stages of group development (Tuckman, 1965) and group behaviour (Bion, 1961).

Reynolds (1994) discusses the broader cultural and individual contexts and their relevance to group projects, in what he describes as the "learning community" (ibid, p.117). This combines an appreciation of how groups reflect social processes, and where programmes "help students make sense of their learning" (ibid, p.117). This approach encourages tutors and students to share in the processes of decision making and the direction of content; it also allows individuals to take responsibility for identifying and meeting their learning needs, and to see themselves and their skillset as a helpful resource within the community. Students are thus enabled to make choices relevant to their individual needs while contributing to each other's learning (ibid, p.117). Here Reynolds identifies the appeal for vocational or professionally driven programmes where learning is directly relevant to work.

LaPrairie's (2007) research into group dynamics and personality characteristics is situated within the frame of behavioural psychology, which she applies to media education. She investigates the factors that contribute to low participation in groups in media education and the conditions in which groups thrive, drawing on psychometric tests used in business, such as the Myers-Briggs Type Indicator® (MBTI) and Emergenetics® (LaPrairie 2007, p.1). She suggests the effects of group learning depend on group organisation and positive participative student leadership (ibid, p.7). She acknowledges that teachers are often not trained in group-learning strategies despite the prevalence of group learning from primary through to further and higher education (Johnson and Johnson, 2002). LaPrairie points to the success of individual accountability within groups, which can be encouraged by assessing individual performance and sharing results. She suggests this also deters *social loafing* (Johnson and Johnson, 1994), where individuals allow others in the group to take on the burden of responsibilities; the *lone-wolf* (Barr et al., 2005) work style, where an individual works for him or herself rather than towards the good of the group, is also discouraged (LaPrairie 2007, p.13).

LaPrairie's work complements Aggarwal and O'Brien (2008), who investigate group work in media education focusing on strategies to tackle social loafing. They highlight the problems inherent to group work in media education, where students do not necessarily have a consistently good learning experience. They identify problems associated with group project work, such as students who do not work as part of the group: the lone wolves who prefer to "work alone when making decisions and setting/accomplishing priorities and goals" (Barr et al., 2003, p.205). Other issues arise due to differences of personality and specialisation of tasks, where the "speciali-sation of labor may force group members to work on separate parts of the project without exposure to the full complexity and richness of the project" (Aggarwal and O'Brien 2008, p.2). Group leaders may have a dominating style that hampers the participation of others while, as LaPrairie (2007) also identifies, team members tend to perceive social loafers as not doing their share of the group work.

Aggarwal and O'Brien's research suggests social loafing or "free riding" as an especially important factor in a group's effectiveness, which frequently results in poor experiences of project-based group work. According to Aggarwal and O'Brien (2008, p.2), "It takes only one social loafer in a group to affect the dynamics of the entire group. Social loafers contribute less than their fair share to group effort but reap the benefit of other mem-bers' efforts because of a common grade for the entire group." Aggarwal and O'Brien examine group dynamics and student satisfaction to understand better why some students participate more than others, and what strategies teachers can implement to enable more effective group project work and student satisfaction. They produce hypotheses for successful group working, which centre around issues of group size (small versus large groups), group formation (whether group composition is tutor-assigned or self-selected by students), peer evaluation (students reflecting on and assessing each other's work), perception of grade fairness (how projects and broader marking schemes assess student work) and the scope of projects (their complexity and ambition). Aggarwal and O'Brien (2008) stress the overall importance of active management by a group's tutor, which, accordingly, will reflect the tutor's individual style and personality.

Hanney (2013) and Hanney and Savin-Baden (2013) further address the problematic nature of group work in project-based work, and in media education directed towards vocational, work-based learning. Hanney (2013) places problem encounters at the heart of project-based learning as pedagogy. Rather than adopting Buckingham (2003) and Berger and McDougall's (2013) scepticism of vocational training within media edu-cation, Hanney (2013, p.44) argues that "creative capabilities cannot be separated from professional capabilities". He calls on educators to embrace the vocational within practice-based media education, and suggests that learning is successfully achieved through the problem encounters faced by students, such as group dynamics or the challenging scope of a project. The skills students develop, such as managing relationships and negotiating access, are as essential as theory and practical or technical skills. While often hidden and described as transferable, Hanney (2013) argues that students have much to gain from embedded reflection on the process (during the process) and the subtle managing and validation of this as a learning process.

Hanney (2013) reminds us that higher education institutions and employers (in creative industries) value practice-based learning, where education constructs "situated learning opportunities" (Kane, 2007) that offer real-world challenges. A master/apprentice model for much practice-based learning is ineffective or insufficient when faced with creative media education that requires students to develop creativity, innovation, and self-expression, alongside group and social skills of cooperation and collaboration (Hanney, 2013). This mirrors professional practice, but within an educational context he suggests the key is in emphasising the learning experience over the professional practice (Hanney, 2013). For Hanney, the key is in problem-based learning, an approach using the inherent problems within projects as a way to promote independent learning. This approach suggests a focus beyond the time-based, project-specific encounter, and instead embeds reflection on the process throughout. Assessment mirrors this ongoing reflection, which is used to enhance production development.

This brief review of theoretical approaches to practical group projects in media education emphasises the importance of considering the broader contexts of learning, and how these can be negotiated and incorporated into strategies for teaching. In this regard Hanney (2013), Reynolds (1994) and Aggarwal and O'Brien (2008) embrace group projects as learning processes that are vocational and ongoing. The survey of student experience discussed in this chapter addresses some of the broader contexts affecting group work, and assesses their impact on the effectiveness of group projects as a form of learning.

Group production survey: methodology

Drawing on Kolb's (1984) theory of experiential learning, which is adapted by Reynolds (1994), this study sought to explore the processes of student learning in group-production projects. It aimed to assess student satisfaction, while gaining a broader picture of the positive and negative challenges they encounter. The study evaluated students' experiences and addressed factors affecting group projects, as suggested in the literature by Reynolds (1994), Aggarwal and O'Brien (2008) and LaPrairie (2007). It then applied these factors to a survey of media production students.

The survey employed qualitative and quantitative methods to examine the learning experiences of undergraduate students who were engaged in practical media production group projects at a Scottish university during the academic year 2014–2015. A total of 67 students, who were enrolled on three media production modules as part of degree programmes at SQA Level 8, 9, and 10, were asked to contribute to the survey. Ethical approval was sought and granted through the university hosting the students and the research. The survey respected confidentiality and participant recruitment and participation was voluntarily conducted with informed consent (Rossman and Rallis, 2003). It was completed at the end of class time and no compensation was offered for participation. The researcher, who was a tutor on several, but not all, of the production-based modules relevant to the study, gained clearance from the programme leaders of relevant subjects.

The sample comprised males and females, UK and international students. All students enrolled on the chosen modules were asked to contribute. Twenty-two of the 67 students completed the survey, which took the form of a questionnaire. The data analysed is based on their responses.

Students were asked to answer questions relevant to "a group project on which you have participated during the last year". They were asked to consider group work from either factual, entertainment, or drama projects across film and television production modules. Questions were grouped into sections – group production, group roles, and the production process. The questions chosen within the survey were influenced by issues raised in the literature review and from the author's experience of supervising and leading group projects. This had raised questions regarding what factors influenced successful group work on practical projects. The questions were directed towards students' experiences and sought their perspectives on the learning process. They also reflected factors suggested by Aggarwal and O'Brien (2008) and LaPrairie (2007) influencing group work projects, such as group size, group formation, peer evaluation, perceptions of grade fairness, and the scope of the project.

The survey combined questions directed towards a yes or no answer, such as *Did the group hold regular meetings?* together with questions requiring a scaled response, such as *On a scale of 1–7, where 1 = "extremely dissatisfied" to 7 = "extremely satisfied", how would you rate your satisfaction with other group members' contributions?* Respondents could also comment or expand on their answers, and were asked questions requiring description or explanation, such as *Which aspect of the production process worked most smoothly and why?*

The collected data were analysed within an interpretive framework (O'Reilly, 2005) with an emphasis on the qualitative commentaries informing a statistical analysis of responses. This chapter acknowledges that the survey data is based on a small sample, and therefore that the statistics reflect a snapshot rather than a broader picture. The research adopts a post-positivist approach (Ryan, 2006) that admits the subjectivity of the researcher and her role in the research endeavour.

Group production survey: results and analysis

Survey analysis draws on both quantitative statistics and qualitative comments and feedback from students. While the statistics reflect a picture at a given moment in time, the comments allow for a more nuanced insight into the students' experiences. The comments selected below are from a range of students, and are reproduced here in the context of the questions they accompanied.

Overall, the results of the survey demonstrated a high level of student satisfaction with group projects as learning experiences. 86% rated their experience as *excellent* or *good* on the group production project.

Vocational learning

Despite Buckingham's (2013) and Berger and McDougall's (2013) concerns about the meaningfulness of vocational courses, the students' responses reflected their appreciation of group work in preparation for industry-associated working contexts. Comments demonstrated a sense of understanding that the group project was a process mirroring future experience in the work place, and that this was a useful and necessary preparation for employment. When asked *In your experience, is group production a useful part of your learning at University? If so, please say why; and if not, why not?* one student responded:

> Yes, it helps you engage with others and experience what working in the real industry would be like.

Similarly, another student appreciated that the group process prepared them for future working conditions:

> I think this is a very useful part in getting to work with others in a realistic situation, taking on different roles and generally working as a team.

Students recognised the vocational skills and knowledge they gained, while appreciating group production as a form of learning, as in the comment:

> Yes, I believe experience and practice is the best way to improve as this is how it would be in the industry, and it makes you work harder as others are relying on you.

Students' comments suggest they understood how the group experience informs their own individual working styles and how they work in groups. One student was clear about how the learning process connected with her career aspirations:

> Yes – to work in television, it is critical to work with groups outside your comfort zone […] I think that group production is very useful; it teaches you how to work as part of a team who are all aiming towards the same goal.

Value and group dynamics: marking, meetings, leadership, roles, and size

The results of the survey corresponded with the strategy promoted by LaPrairie (2007) of sharing accountability between the group and the individual. 68% of students found the assessment process to be fair, with 62% indicating they were assessed for both group and individual contributions. As Aggarwal and O'Brien (2008) suggest, a perception of a fair marking system incorporating the group's work is an important factor in successful group learning.

Students in the survey responded positively to being part of groups that held regular meetings, had strong leaders, and where they felt valued as members of their group. They appreciated having roles and responsibilities clearly demarcated, with 91% indicating members of their group worked towards a shared goal. This echoes LaPrairie's (2007, p.12) suggestion that teachers could promote positive interdependence within learning groups by establishing a clear group goal around which students can unite.

Students did not indicate issues with members not taking on their share of the workload, such as LaPrairie's (2007) and Aggarwal and O'Brien's (2008) social loafers, and most were satisfied with other group members' contributions. Regular meetings went hand in hand with a sense of valued participation, with a high proportion indicating that individual contributions to discussion were valued.

While Aggarwal and O'Brien (2008) indicate group size is often a factor influencing group harmony, suggesting smaller groups work better, the survey suggested that this was in fact not a determining factor; students worked positively in a range of group sizes, with a majority of groups numbering over 6 members. It would seem that the presence of other supporting indicators – such as regular meetings, perception of fair marking, and an environment where students felt their contribution was valued – ensures that group size need not be an overriding issue.

Respondents who indicated their role lacked value, or who did not always have enough to do during projects, tended to suggest this was due to a combination of group size and the specialisation of roles. For students who felt they did not contribute enough, this featured as a common reason, as exemplified in the following comment:

> Many roles were specific to pre or post production and because of the size of the group those people had very little to do during the production.

Another student expressed a lack of purpose and value within the group:

> My role was extremely easy and basically pointless.

This experience contrasted with other students, who were not held back by the role specialisation. Comments such as the following indicated that some were able to make the most of their role, and recognised their worth as part of the group effort.

> I feel that once I did my part I didn't have as strong a role, but was still necessary.

Similarly, where groups were small, there were opportunities to assume other roles, such as for a student who indicated that if he was not busy with his chosen role, he helped out in other areas.

The complexity of the project (Aggarwal and O'Brien, 2008) was not articulated as an issue but, together with group size and role specialisation, may have created difficulties of engagement and participation to some students.

Tutor's role and student agency

86% of students responded that they did not believe the tutor could have done any more to manage the group. The student survey indicated an even mixture of responses around group selection, from tutor-assigned groups, student-selected and a combination of the two. The survey confirmed what Aggarwal and O'Brien observed: "Research has also shown that when individuals voluntarily commit to membership in a group, they are more inclined to show group solidarity" (2008, p.4). Groups that presented positive outcomes did so because the participants had responsibility and agency in the creation of the group. This also allows successful working relations to develop from one project to another (Hanney, 2013), which is important for ongoing learning and for the development of vocational professionalism.

Group make-up

59% of students were satisfied with the gender and age balance of production groups. There were no further comments relating to this question, but the 41% of students who perceived an imbalance in the make-up of the groups suggests this is an area for further attention. The results and analysis point towards a generally positive experience for students engaging with production projects. Students enrolled on the courses surveyed appreciated the vocational dimension to group learning. Some students navigated the complexities of group production and roles better than others, and where pro-active management of the group process was in place, students worked effectively in their groups.

Conclusion

This study has investigated both general and specific examples of group learning in media education. It has served to highlight a range of approaches to this area of pedagogy, and some of the key factors relevant within its context. The survey demonstrates group work in media education as a positive learning experience for students, as they appreciate its short-term and longer-term value within their education and for starting a career in the industry. While the survey suggested students were mostly satisfied with the learning and teaching approaches to group work, the instances where there was discord or dissatisfaction are revealing.

This chapter suggests that students are responsive to teaching and learning strategies that facilitate group project learning in media education. These strategies should be responsive to the broader social contexts of student learning, and are best applied when considered as part of ongoing processes continuing into an individual's working life. The strategies identified within this chapter reflect that the tutor (and the programme overall) actively manage groups, while still allowing students the agency and responsibility to encounter and solve problems.

In group work, the needs of the individual remain strong, and require the attention of a tutor to manage or facilitate leadership where there is opportunity for all to contribute. The organisation and management of groups across the production process is critical, balancing real-life vocational training with tutor-led support. This approach ensures opportunities to learn and make mistakes at all stages of the project. Critical reflection throughout the course of group projects, through assessment or group meetings, is a positive strategy in enhancing learning. Students appreciate the production project as part of an ongoing, iterative, and active cycle embedding the learning experience within the goal of professional practice.

This chapter is based on a survey of students' learning experiences, and is contextualised by a literature review relevant to practical group production projects and media education. It endorses early intervention strategies to identify and support groups where individuals are contributing less, or slipping into lone wolf or social loafing patterns. Students surveyed in this survey did not perceive other students within those categories, but a small number did identify themselves as contributing less, or being in roles which were worth less than others. Identifying the reasons for these circumstances is crucial if all students are to be treated equally within group project work.

This chapter suggests the specialisation of roles within media production projects as a key factor in effective group working and student satisfaction. How this is managed within the group, along with shared responsibilities and leadership, is also an important factor. Research suggests that students *want* to be involved in productions, and that they find the greatest satisfaction when given a degree of their own agency in terms of group selection.

Survey analysis suggests further areas of enquiry and recommendations for future research. The methodology employed has combined survey with literature review; further research would encompass a broader scope for both. The chapter acknowledges the limitations of the survey and its small sample size. It recognises that respondents are perhaps overly weighted with those who did have positive experiences and who are reflecting on production modules designed to accommodate practical group learning.

The survey has highlighted further questions around how students carry out production roles in groups. Are there differences between genres of production within television and film production? Does the genre of production (for example factual, fiction or entertainment) affect group learning?

Wider recommendations for research would also include a broader investigation into diversity within group organisation, such as across age, gender, background, and ethnicity. This was considered only briefly in this study due to constraints of time and resources. The chapter would recommend further research to include teachers' perspectives on group learning and education, considering their experiences and perceptions of student learning and management. Further research should also consider the effectiveness of group projects in relation to vocational training, with reflection from former students on whether this approach to learning prepared them for employment in the creative industries. Students perceive group projects as beneficial for their future – to what extent can we measure this to be the case? This could also be cross-referenced with data on the employment of former students following higher education.

This chapter substantiates the view that group learning through practical production projects is essential within media education, and suggests this approach to teaching and learning deserves continuing critical research to ensure the highest levels of student experience and success.

Dr Kirsten MacLeod is a Lecturer in Television and Film in the School of Arts and Creative Industries at Edinburgh Napier University. She is a practising film-maker with a background in factual television, visual anthropology, and community media. She has a PhD from the University of the West of Scotland in Creative Media Practice, based on practice-led participatory media production fieldwork in Scottish communities. Her research interests include epistemology and practice in participatory and alternative media, documentary production, women in production, practice-led and participatory methodologies, and media education pedagogy.

References

Aggarwal, P. and O'Brien, C. L. (2008). Social loafing on group projects: structural antecedents and effect on student satisfaction. *Journal of Marketing Education*, 30 (3), 255–264.

Barr, T. F., Dixon, A. L., and Gassenheimer, J. B. (2005). Exploring the "lone wolf" phenomenon in student teams. *Journal of Marketing Education*, 27 (1), 81–90.

Barr, T. F., Dixon, A. L., and Gassenheimer, J. B. (2003), Identifying the lone wolf: a team perspective. *Journal of Personal Selling and Sales Management*, 23 (3), 205–219.

Berger, R. and McDougall, J. (2013). What is media education for? *Media Education Research Journal*, 3 (1), 5–20.

Bion, W. R. (1961). *Experiences in Groups New York*. New York: Basic Books.

Buckingham, D. (2003), *Media Education: Literacy, Learning and Contemporary Culture*. Cambridge: Polity Press.

Buckingham, D. (2013). Teaching the creative class? Media education and the media industries in the age of "participatory culture". *Journal of Media Practice*, 14 (1), 25–41.

Buckingham, D., Grahame, J., and Sefton-Greene, J. (1995). *Making Media: Practical Production in Media Education*. London: English and Media Centre.

Dewey, J. (1916) *Democracy and Education*. New York: Macmillan.

Ettington, D. and Camp, R. (2002). Facilitating transfer of skills between group projects and work teams. *Journal of Management Education*, 26 (4), 356–79.

Hanney, R. (2013) Towards a situated media practice: reflections on the implementation of project-led problem-based learning. *Journal of Media Practice*, 14 (1), 43–59.

Hanney, R. and Savin-Baden, M. (2013). The problem of projects: understanding the theoretical underpinnings of project-led PBL. *London Review of Education*, 11 (1), 7–19.

Johnson, D. W. and Johnson, R. T. (1994). An overview of co-operative learning. In: Thousand, J., Villa, A., and Nevin, A. (Eds.). *Creativity and Collaborative Learning*, Baltimore: Brookes Press.

Johnson, D. W. and Johnson, R. T. (2002). Co-operative learning and social interdependence theory. In: Tindale, R. S. et al. (Eds.). *Theory and Research on Small Groups*. Plenum Press: New York, 9–35.

Kane, G. (2007). Step-by-step: A model for practice-based learning. *Journal of Continuing Education in the Health Professions*, 27 (4), 220–26.

Kolb, D. (2014). *Experiential Learning: Experience as the Source of Learning and Development*. London: Financial Times, Prentice-Hall.

Kolb, D. A. (1984). *Experiential Learning: Experience as the Source of Learning and Development*. Englewood Cliffs, NJ: Prentice-Hall.

Kolb, D. A. and Fry, R. (1975). Towards an applied theory of experiential learning. In: Cooper, C. L. (Ed.). *Theories of Group Processes*. New York: Wiley, 33–58.

LaPrairie, K. N. (2007). *Using Group Dynamics and Personality Characteristics to Form Learning Groups in High School Multimedia Courses*. PhD. Thesis, University of Louisiana at Lafayette.

O'Reilly, K. (2005). *Ethnographic Methods*, London: Routledge.

Reynolds, M. (1994/2013). *Group Work in Education and Training*, London: Kogan Page.

Rossman, G. and Rallis, S. F. (2003). *Learning in the Field: An Introduction to Qualitative Research* (2nd ed.). *San Francisco*: Jossey-Bass Publishers.

Ryan, A. B. (2006). Post-positivist approaches to research. In: Antonesa, M., Fallon, H., Ryan, A. B., Walsh, T. and Borys, L. *Researching and Writing Your Thesis: A Guide for Postgraduate Students*. Maynooth: MACE, 12–26.

Savin-Baden, M. (2000). *Problem-Based Learning in Higher Education: Untold Stories*. Buckingham, UK: Society for Research in Higher Education and Open University Press.

Savin-Baden, M. (2007). *A Practical Guide to Problem-based Learning*. London: Routledge.

Treisman, P. U. (1985). *A Study of the Mathematics Performance of Black Students at the University of California, Berkeley*. Unpublished PhD. Thesis, University of California, Berkeley.

Tuckman, B. W. (1965). Developmental sequence in small groups. *Psychological Bulletin*, 63 (6), 384.

Wales, C. E. and Sager, R. (1978). *The Guided Design Approach*. Englewood Cliffs, NJ: Educational Technology.

Contextualising information literacy to assessment criteria: a collaborative approach

Keith Walker and Stephen Robertson

ABSTRACT

This chapter explores the collaboration between a subject librarian and a module leader with the aim of improving the information literacy skills of students within two cohorts of students on an undergraduate business module. Generic library resources were replaced by bespoke material within the module assessment handbook. The study reported in the chapter used cohort analysis to explore the impact of these changes: specifically, students' use of the material provided and the impact on their grades. Data was collected from the module's online presence, which allows an accurate measure of how often students make use of the tools provided and when in the trimester this happens. It also examines assessment results, with the aim of establishing a link between tool usage and cohort performance. The findings show that students' use of tools can be improved through better signposting, with the timing of that usage appearing to be linked to assessment deadlines. There was a slight improvement in grade when the tools provided were module-specific. Recommendations include involving students in the development and review of information literacy skills materials and engagement with other module leaders and subject librarians to provide a more consistent approach to information literacy across programmes of study.

Keywords: information literacy, assessment criteria, technology-enhanced learning

Introduction

The aim of this chapter is to explore students' use of bespoke information literacy materials prepared jointly by the teaching staff and the subject librarian. The specific focus here is the level of student use of the time-sensitive bespoke research resources recommended in the assessment handbook by the module leader and the subsequent impact on the quality of the work submitted. The results from this analysis allow for focused efforts in future material development.

The collaboration giving rise to the development of the materials in question grew from a long-running conversation between researchers who shared an interest in the information literacy of students; particularly, in their use of digital sources. The module leader had observed over a period of several years that the majority of students did not make sufficient use of library materials in assignments: they tended to use generic web search engines to locate their sources, instead of library versions with the added function of results restricted to academic sources. The subject librarian shared this frustration despite the creation of web-based resources. These included short-form videos that were automatically included on the Virtual Learning Environment (VLE) presence for each module, but which had limited information on how to use these resources in relation to specific assignments.

The authors sought to combine their complementary skillsets with the shared goal of developing the information literacy skills of students. They would achieve this by clearly linking assessment criteria with library resources before assessing the impact on the students' grades. The first stage of the collaboration was to establish a method, which would provide an answer to the questions: do the students use the material provided, and does that translate into an improved performance?

Context and rationale

The concept of co-created web-based information literacy resources embedded within the VLE is not new. There have been calls for greater collaboration between academic and library staff to develop resources together rather than working in isolation (Dalal & Lackie, 2014; Easter, Bailey and Klages, 2014; Browning, 2015). Studies tend to focus on new members of academic staff raising awareness of the available resources (Bausman, Ward and Pell, 2014), or on increasing the number of sessions run by librarians within modules (Black, Crest and Volland, 2001). The focus of this project differs from those studies carried out in other institutions by examining which resources were used at which point in the term by students. This is achieved through analysis of the logs created by the VLE each time an item is accessed. The context of this study can be viewed from three perspectives: the module leader, who sets and grades the assessment tools; the subject librarian, with responsibility for the development of a collection that contains the appropriate resources; and the student who seeks to join the assessment and to access the resources to complete the set task. New tools to support different ways of learning can be developed through formal and informal collaboration between the three participants, as each brings a different skillset to the conversation (Monge & Frisicaro-Pawlowski, 2014). "Deliberate and thoughtful scaffolding of information literacy instruction" (ibid, p.71) helps students develop the skills required for the information age. The responsibility for the scaffolding lies with the module leader and subject librarian, but the focus should be on student need (Minocha, Schroeder & Schneider, 2011).

When students search for information, knowing where to look is paramount, as the plethora of business information available can overwhelm students. Thus, intervention by a subject librarian and the module leader can assist in helping the students understand the sources available to them (Leigh and Gibbon 2008, p.516). Previous studies have shown that students prefer to use other sources; in particular, freely available sources found through online search engines such as Google. This is the case even despite academic libraries having access to corporate business databases and intelligence (Bain, 2004). Students then compound the poor evaluation of sources by demonstrating an inability, or unwillingness, to critically evaluate their findings. Cunningham (2003) goes as far as to say that "business students are seemingly some of the most [over-confident] of all library patron groups when it comes to accessing, selecting, and evaluating online information. Often, they assume everything they need is accessible through a quick search on Google or another favorite search engine. At times this naiveté and overconfidence in the web leads to frustration when results of a search do not measure up."

It has been suggested that academic staff assume that students have the necessary skills, then go on to express frustration when submitted work does not reach the required standard (Sanabria, 2013). Sanabria argues that this disconnect between expectation and reality creates an opportunity for module leaders and subject librarians to work together more closely to co-create assignments that match outcomes with the available resources. Library collection builders need to understand if and how resources are going to be used, as this influences purchasing decisions, lending a financial imperative to collaboration (Browning, 2015) to ensure that the resources available match the assignment set (Bain, 2004).

To ensure effective collaboration, a joint vocabulary is required between the participants so that a long-term, continuously-improving relationship can be developed (Gardner & White-Farnham, 2013). The Society of College, National and University Libraries (SCONUL) identified seven information literacy skills that should be encouraged in students (see figure 1, overleaf) that they describe as the Seven Pillars (SCONUL, 2013).

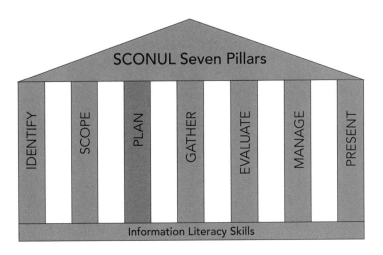

Figure 1: Developed from SCONUL, 2013.

Identify maps to understanding "differences between information environments in academic and enterprise settings" (SCONUL 2016, p.1), so that the student is then able to "recognise the nature and forms taken by information/data that are needed to help resolve business questions or problems..." (ibid). *Plan* and *gather* reflects the importance of time management when searching for information and the need to focus on searching: being able to ask the right questions and to use the correct keywords when searching for the information required (ibid, p.3). Equally important is the need to *evaluate* the information retrieved, and to think critically and analytically about the results of the search. For example: Is the source reputable? Is it accurate? Does it answer the question properly? Is there bias (ibid, p.4)? Finally, the student must be aware of *managing* and *presenting* the information that they have retrieved properly. This means correctly citing and referencing sources within the piece of work. All of the above is important in an academic scenario, but equally so in the business world.

These seven skills apply to all forms of physical and digital research (SCONUL, 2013), and have been extended to Graduate Employability (SCONUL, 2016). This maps across the original pillars and contextualises them in the business environment. As well as providing students the basic tools to complete their assessment, the skills are contextualised to a business setting. Information literacy in the assessment criteria becomes important, not just for the life of the assessment, but also as a skillset to prepare for and to take into the world of employment.

Description of activity

With the above taken into consideration, what was required was to guide the students: explaining to them how they could find the right information, how they could then use the systems they were guided to, and finally how to use the resulting content found. To reduce variable factors, data from two cohorts of students on the same module over consecutive years (n=255 and n=269) were analysed to measure the impact of the changes made. The module chosen drew participants from a range of undergraduate business programmes, which allowed the authors to widen the focus of the study from a single source.

Previously, links to information sources and library guides were in a block on the VLE module homepage (see figure 2).

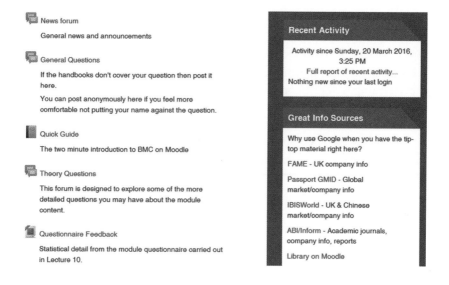

Figure 2: Moodle design prior to change.

To make the links between the assessment criteria and the resources available in the library collection more clear to students, these elements of information literacy skills were embedded within the module Assessment Handbook (see figure 3, overleaf).

Students on this module had to prepare a group presentation focusing on a single company, as assigned to them by the module leader. In ten minutes, the group had to present their analysis of a company, with the following

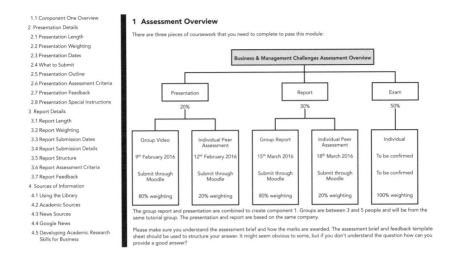

Figure 3: Moodle design Cohort 2.

information: what the firm does, where it is based, an analysis of whether it is performing well or poorly, and how that might be defined. This required a good range of data that was relevant to the company. Twenty percent of the final mark was for sources used.

Within the Module Assessment Handbook there is a section entitled Sources of Information (see figure 3) which has five subsections:

- Using the Library
- Academic Sources
- News Sources
- Google News
- Developing Academic Research Skills for Business

The first four sections are links to various online resources, generic library pages, links to relevant academic databases and greater direction to free access web sources, such as Google News to find up-to-date press stories.

The new embedded area with greater value is the Developing Academic Research Skills for Business section. In this, the links between the assessment criteria and information literacy skills were made explicit. Although the SCONUL Pillars were implied in the assessment criteria, there was no direct link to the library resources. Fifteen percent of the report marks were awarded based on the sources and use of information within the group exercise. The marking criteria within the module were explicit in the need to gather evidence from good sources of information within the assessment. On reflection, the assumption made by the module leader was that the students already knew how to gather and evaluate the required data. The submitted coursework, however, suggested that students were in fact not aware of how to use the Seven Pillars to underpin their coursework. In order to improve the digital literacy of the students on the module, short-form videos were created by the subject librarian to guide the students through the process of gathering and evaluating high-quality data. These films were as follows:

- How to find academic journal articles in ABI/Inform Business Database
- How to evaluate the information returned from the search

A short multiple-choice quiz was also included to assist students in developing their referencing skills.

As part of the collaboration, the module leader and the subject librarian reviewed student usage of the resources by Cohort 1. The Assessment Handbook moved from the Module Introduction folder into a specific section on the assessment (see figure 4) to integrate the library resources into the assessment, rather than it existing as a separate entity.

▼ Assessment Details

Details of the assessment groups.

Use the email address provide to make contact with the others in the group. Start researching your company using the detail provided as a starting point.

Check the marking criteria, set a meeting, agree tasks and get started as soon as possible.

Assessment Handbook

Use this to understand what the assessments are, when you are required to do it and what you have to do to pass.

General Diagram

JPEG version of the Boddy framework for you to use in the reports.

Finding Business Information

This is a recording of a webinar that looks at the resources to use when looking for company information, market information and economic data. Developed by Keith Walker from the library.

Company list

This term's company list. The articles given are there to give you a little background into the company. The Assessment Handbook has a lot more detail on finding high quality information.

▼ Assessment Submission

Section for assessment submission.

Figure 4: Moodle design academic session Cohort 2.

A short video clip named *Finding Business Information* was created, demonstrating the relevant non-academic business databases that could be used for data collection. These included the FAME database from Bureau Van Dijk and Passport GMID from Euromonitor. The search terms in the examples used the companies that were given to the students, making the examples more relevant than a simple how-to video. This was a further development of bespoke resources focusing on the specific, in order that the relevance of the resources might become clearer in the context of the assessment. Originally, the authors had discussed customising one of the tutorial sessions to cover information-gathering. However, with ten classes in a week, this was not possible; thus, the video was created. This audio-visual content was consistent with the class delivery, as a range of podcasts is a key part of the module design. The comparison of the two student cohorts forms the basis of the study contained in the next section of the chapter.

Findings

The study compared two cohorts of the module. Although the module runs in both trimesters, the comparison is made using a relative, consistent group of programmes represented in the cohorts to reduce the variable factors in the study. With regards to students' use of the materials, a comparison was made (see figure 5) of the proportion of students accessing the Sources of Information chapter in the Assessment Handbook at any point in the term.

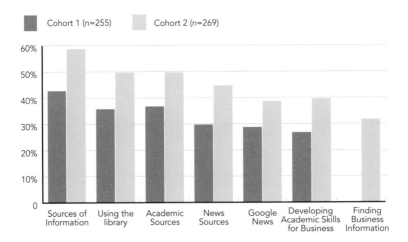

Figure 5: Handbook page usage by cohort.

This analysis suggests that moving the pages from the Introduction Section on Moodle to the Assessment Section had a positive impact on the number of students referencing the material. In Cohort 2, a higher proportion of students made use of the resources, although there is a similar pattern with fewer students reading subsequent pages. However, the positive impact of the location change is that the proportion of students reading the sections on *Using the Library* and *Academic Sources* increased from around one-third of the class to almost half. This would appear to indicate that better signposting along with a clear link between the assessment criteria and the online resources can encourage students to make use of academic sources in their coursework. On average, 14% more students accessed the *Sources of Information* pages within the Assessment Handbook in Cohort 2 than had done in Cohort 1, which suggests that the collaborative approach to the material creation had an impact.

Over 30% of the class made use of the *Finding Business Information* video included on the VLE. This link was not included as part of the Handbook but was provided as a stand-alone link in the Assessment section within Moodle (see figure 4). The availability of the link, and the customised nature of the content, were signposted in the lectures and tutorials. It should be noted that as the related assessment is a group activity, there is a possibility that one or two students per group used the video and shared the details with their colleagues, although we have no data with which to back up this suggestion.

Having established that students do make use of these resources, a second analysis was carried out on the data to establish when in the trimester students make use of these resources (see figure 6).

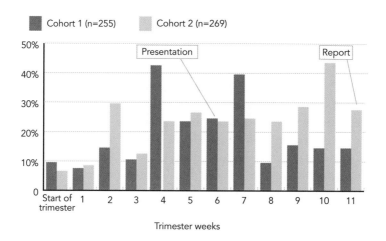

Figure 6: Cohort 1 versus Cohort 2 Handbook Resource usage by week.

This second analysis plots when in the term students make use of the library resources from the Assessment Handbook. The Y-axis indicates the proportion of the total students who referenced those pages. Week "0" is used to indicate those students who accessed the material on Moodle before the term began. The decision to cut the graph at Week 11 was based on when the coursework was due. From Week 12 onwards, the module focus is on the exam, and specific audio-visual material is made available for the students.

Between the two cohorts there are significant differences in the pattern of usage. In Cohort 2 there is more use of the Handbook pages in Week 2 than in Cohort 1. The Assessment Handbooks are given as pre-class reading although in Cohort 2 some details of class usage were shared in the introductory lecture, which may have encouraged some students to make use of the material after the class.

In Cohort 1 the main usage peaks were in Week 4 (42% of students accessed the pages), which is when the assessment groups were published and teams were required to create their initial presentation. The second spike was in Week 7 (39%), which is when presentation feedback was made available. The Making Feedback Work For You sessions, provided by a specialist team within the University using the module feedback, appears to have prompted some of the students to revisit the assessment criteria and, in particular, the library resources pages. Following that there is limited use of the pages, with around 15% of the class making use of them.

The pattern in Cohort 2 is markedly different. The resources were used by around 25% of the class between Weeks 4 and 8, with a slight increase in Week 9 (28%) before the peak of Week 10 (43%), which was the week before the group report was due. This would suggest that students are making more use of the library resources pages in the run-up to the report: this may be in response to the feedback given on the group presentation.

The comparison of the Assessment Handbook pages (see figure 6) provides relatively little information, though, as Session Cohort 2 saw the introduction of the video material that was directly linked to from within Moodle.

The *Finding Business Information* video was made available in Week 5 and signposted in the tutorials that week. The reaction of the students to this type of resource appears positive, with 40% of the cohort accessing the material in the first week. The second week saw 27% of the class accessing the video, and, although usage did drop immediately after the presentation was submitted, the subsequent weeks before the report hand-in saw usage slowly increase again. Students did, however, appear more comfortable with the links embedded in the Assessment Handbook. In Week 10, 43% of students used the Assessment Handbook pages, compared with 24% watching the video.

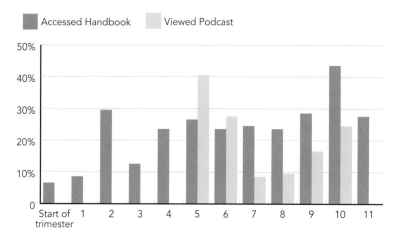

Figure 7: Cohort 1 resource usage by week.

These figures suggest that students are discerning when it comes to selecting the most appropriate resource, which is consistent with previous research (Conole et al., 2008; Harris & Park 2008). Figure 8 combines the data from figure 7 to allow a direct comparison with Session Cohort 1, where only the Assessment Handbook links were included.

Figure 8 shows that there was a spike in resource usage in Week 5 (57% in Cohort 2, compared with 23% the previous year) and Week 10 (59%, compared with 14%).

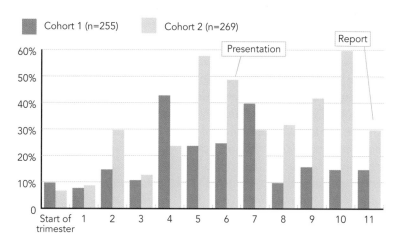

Figure 8: Cohort 1 versus Cohort 2 combined resource usage by week.

In Cohort 1 there was limited use of the resources between the presentation and the report; in Cohort 2 there was a steady growth from Week 7 (31%) to Week 10 (59%). The data in figure 8 would appear to suggest that the combination of resources encourages more students to use the links to the library resources. In addition to the introduction of the bespoke video material, the improved placement of the Assessment Handbook and greater signposting in class appears to have encouraged more students to make greater use of the resources with the highest spike in usage the week before the two assessments were due.

The second question in the introduction considers a positive impact on student performance in the assessments, so a comparison of assessment feedback between the cohorts was carried out. Both elements of the assessment award marks for the use of appropriate data as a basis for analysis of the company. In the presentation this equates to 20% of the marks; in the report, 15%. Figure 9 shows a comparison of the median grades for these two components in Cohort 1 and Cohort 2.

	Presentation			Report		
	Weight	Median	Percentage	Weight	Median	Percentage
Cohort 1	20%	18	60%	15%	7	46.7%
Cohort 2	20%	15	50%	15%	8	53.3%

Figure 9: Data usage grades by group.

This analysis shows that although the median presentation mark for data usage dropped from one year to the next, there was a slight improvement in the report element. One change from Cohort 1 to Cohort 2 was the move from a live presentation in class to the submission of a video by each group. The content of the presentation was identical between the cohorts, with only the mode of delivery changed. This may, however, have had an impact on the marking, as the recorded presentation allows for greater scrutiny of the data and how they were used in the presentation. The *Finding Business Information* video was used by students but this may have been recorded too late for the students to adjust their presentation although there is no evidence to support this supposition. It would appear that the improved resources and signposting had a positive impact on the use of data within the report.

The end-of-term questionnaire, administered by the module leader, returned little data of value on the student view of the library podcast.

Around one-third of the respondents indicated that they had viewed the resource, which is consistent with the VLE logs. Of the 96 students who answered the question (a response rate of 36%), only nine students added a comment about the resource, providing little additional data on how or why students made use of the video or not.

Future developments

The data collected show that the collaborative approach has increased access to the library resources. However, it may be that the material needs better signposting, or indeed a change of name to make it more relevant to the students. The way in which the assessment criteria are linked to the Seven Pillars also requires some development. As stated in the introduction, this is an ongoing study; comparisons between cohorts will continue, thus enabling a continued scrutiny of the embedded material and the impact it is having on the students. The work to date has established a method of data collection and comparison to assess the impact of the collaboration on student behaviour.

As new resources are developed, the collaboration will be extended to include the views of third group highlighted in the rationale section: the students. Dalal & Lackie (2014) demonstrate the importance of the student perspective in the creation of online resources. As new resources are developed and the signposting improved within the VLE, the views of students will be sought in the design stage rather than simply to gather data based on web-page hits. The same module will continue to be used for consistency in the data collection, which remains an important facet of the long-term collaboration. The use of survey data, gathered through module questionnaires, will allow a greater depth of information to be gathered by the researchers. The focus will then be expanded from *what* and *when*, gathered from the VLE logs, to include *how* and *why* students made use of the materials. The poor response rate to the specific question at the end of module questionnaire leaves the authors no further forward in understanding this perspective. The inclusion of this third perspective cannot be left until after the event but active engagement with previous students to develop new resources is necessary. More voices need to be added to the conversation.

The analysis of student grades shows a slight increase in the component grade for the sources of information used, suggesting that more investigation is required. Are the resources appropriate? Do students understand how to translate these skills into coursework? Do they know how to present their findings in a way that makes the most of the material gathered? By extending this collaboration to include students, these new questions can be addressed.

Recommendations

Although the resources were specifically designed for a single business module, the concept of collaboration is transferable. As the initial study covers a second year core module, it would be beneficial to roll out a similar approach on other core modules with the programme at different stages of study. This would allow a consistent approach of embedded information and digital literacy skills throughout the career of the student, with the gradual increase in skills over the duration of the programme. This would result in a student cohort who use information literacies as a matter of course, with these skills being used as second nature. The intention would be not only to create higher quality coursework, but also to give these students the information and digital literacy skills required to become a success in the burgeoning digital economy. Similarly, this approach is not unique to business and management courses. All academic research and study requires use of resources; information and digital literacies are necessary for success. Embedding links connected to assessments to contextualise their importance for the student cohort is not a subject-specific approach, and can be altered to relate to resources and information that is relevant to what is being taught.

Conclusion

The process of writing this chapter has given the authors the opportunity to reflect on the ongoing collaboration to develop the information literacy skills of their students. The chapter began with two questions: do the students use the information literacy material provided, and does that translate into improved performance? Through interrogation of the Moodle logs, the chapter outlines a method for answering the first of these questions. The placement of the material within the VLE making the links between assessment and the available information clear appears to have had a positive impact on student behaviour. By placing the library resources within the assessment information within the module it appears that more students can be encouraged to make use of the material.

Keith Walker is the Subject Librarian for Edinburgh Napier University's Business School and has been so since 2002. He has a strong interest in digital and information literacy and getting it "out there" for students to understand in an academic context, as well as understanding it as an employability skill and a graduate attribute. He enjoys working with academic staff to embed these skills in a holistic approach to the student experience. Until recently, Keith was Chair of the Business Librarians Association.

Stephen Robertson is a Lecturer in Business Management at Edinburgh Napier University. He joined the University in 2008 after the completion of his MBA. Prior to this, Stephen spent almost 20 years in the IT industry during which he led a wide range of project and support teams. This broad experience underpins his creation of a learning environment that extends beyond the classroom using a range of social media to encourage student engagement. Other research interests include the Business of Professional Football in Scotland and cross-cultural interprofessional ethical practice. In his free time, Stephen manages the successful University Football 1st XI.

References

Bain, K. (2004). *What The Best College Teachers Do*. [Kindle] Cambridge, MA. U.S.A.: Harvard University Press.

Bausman, M., Ward, S.L., and Pell, J. (2014). Beyond satisfaction: understanding and promoting the instructor-librarian relationship. *New Review of Academic Librarianship*, 20 (2),117–136.

Black, C., Crest, S., and Volland, M. (2001) Building a successful information literacy infrastructure on the foundation of librarian-faculty collaboration. *Research Strategies,* 18 (3), 215–225.

Browning, S. (2015). The discovery-collection librarian connection: cultivating collaboration for better discovery. *Collection Management*, 40 (4), 197–206.

Conole, G., de Laat, M., Dillon, T. and Darby. J. (2008). 'Disruptive technologies', 'pedagogical innovation': what's new? Findings from an in-depth study of students' use and perception of technology. *Computers and Education*, 50 (2), 511–524.

Cunningham, N. (2003). Information Competency Skills for Business Students. *Academic BRASS* 1(1) [Online]. Available at: http://www.ala.org/rusa/sections/brass/brasspubs/academicbrass/acadarchives/volume1number1/academicbrassv1 [Accessed: 19 February 2016].

Dalal, H. & Lackie, R. (2014). What if you build it and they still won't come? Addressing student awareness of resources and services with promotional videos. *Journal of Library and Information Services in Distance Learning*, 8 (3), 225–241.

Easter, J., Bailey, S., and Klages, G. (2014). Faculty and librarians unite! How two librarians and one faculty member developed an information literacy strategy for distance education students. *Journal of Library and Information Services in Distance Learning*, 8 (3), 242–262.

Gardner, C.C. and White-Farnham, J. (2013). "She has a vocabulary I just don't have": faculty culture and information literacy collaboration. *Collaborative Librarianship*, 5 (4), 235–243.

Harris, H. and Park, S. (2008). Educational usages of podcasting. *British Journal of Educational Technology*, 39 (3), 548–551.

Leigh, J. S. A. and C. A. Gibbon (2008). Information literacy and the introductory management classroom. *Journal of Management Education*, 32 (4), 509–530.

Minocha, S., Schroeder, A., and Schneider, C. (2011). Role of the educator in social software initiatives in further and higher education: a conceptualisation and research agenda. *British Journal of Educational Technology*, 42 (6), 889–903.

Monge, R. and Frisicaro-Pawlowski, E. (2014). Redefining information literacy to prepare students for the 21st-century workforce. *Innovative Higher Education*, 39 (1), 59–73.

Sanabria, J.E. (2013). The librarian and the collaborative design of effective library assignments: recommendations for faculty on question design for student success in research assignments. *Collaborative Librarianship*, 5 (4), 243–246.

SCONUL, (2013). The SCONUL seven pillars of information literacy through a digital literacy 'lens' [Online]. Available at: http://www.sconul.ac.uk/sites/default/files/documents/Digital_Lens.pdf [Accessed: 19 February 2016].

SCONUL, (2016). The graduate employability lens on the SCONUL seven pillars of information literacy [Online]. Available at: http://www.sconul.ac.uk/sites/default/files/documents/Employability_Lens_only_2015_0.pdf [Accessed: 19 February 2016].

3 | Digital technology and innovative practices in the classroom

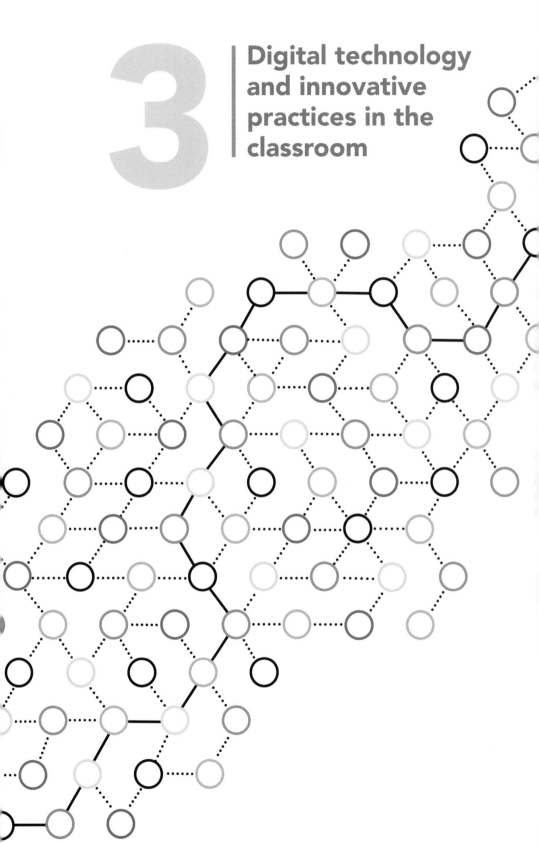

The accidental podcaster

Stephen Robertson and Sarah Sholl

ABSTRACT

The aim of this chapter is to explore podcast use among students, employing longitudinal data from large cohorts to demonstrate to other teachers their potential as a relevant pedagogical tool. The study is novel in that it uses quantitative data from seven large student cohorts, allowing insights into use and relevance that could not be derived accurately from questionnaire data. Moodle-generated data logs from seven consecutive student cohorts were captured and analysed in order to understand the volume, frequency, and pattern of podcast usage at different points in the trimester. Findings show that podcasts are used extensively by students over the trimester and can therefore be considered both relevant and useful. The authors hope this chapter will encourage tutors to value podcasts as pedagogical tools, enabling efficiency of time and consistency of support where it might otherwise be difficult, and facilitating self-reflection as an important part of professional development.

Keywords: podcasts, technology enhanced learning, large cohort teaching, lecture capture

Introduction

Supplementary media are used as tools within learning strategies. However, the way technology has advanced means that they are not used in the standardised fashion one might expect. The term "podcasting" has been in use since 2004 (Hammersley, 2004). It has been identified that students perceive podcasts as beneficial to their learning (Danielson et al., 2014), particularly as a revision tool (Evans, 2008; Lonn and Teasley, 2009; Margaryan et al., 2011).

Various studies have used questionnaires to explore how students use podcasts and how helpful they find them (for example, Carvalho et al., 2009; Scutter et al., 2010; De Villiers and Walsh, 2015). To the authors' knowledge, no study has captured quantitative longitudinal data from large cohorts in order to establish the proportion of students who use podcasts, and when they access those podcasts. These data are useful because they are available for entire cohorts, they are less vulnerable to bias than questionnaire data, and they can be categorised across multiple undergraduate cohorts.

Context and rationale

"Is it okay if I record your classes?" This was asked by Sophie[1], a second-year undergraduate student who had been diagnosed with dyslexia. "Yes, sure," was the answer, "but I'll do the recording for you so that the quality is more consistent as I walk around the room." Thus began the podcasts for one of the largest undergraduate modules in the school.

The next class was recorded using a voice recorder and a lapel microphone. Given the file size, it was too large to be hosted by the existing virtual learning environment (VLE). It was therefore uploaded to an external site and the link sent to the student. Sophie confirmed the sound quality was an improvement upon her own previous recordings, and remarked that the benefit students gain from a lecture is often enhanced by listening back to a recording of it. Throughout the rest of the trimester the lectures continued to be recorded and uploaded, with the external link available to all of the students via the VLE. As time progressed the number of students accessing the files increased.

Towards the end of the trimester, audio recordings of revision classes were split into several smaller files representing different subject areas, so that students could make use of them in a more targeted way. Historically, several revision classes have been held each trimester, with their content being directed by the needs of the students. With the advent of the revision recordings, it was noted that the number of students attending the revision classes was decreasing; some students, however, commented that they still preferred the interactive sessions because of the visual element. The use of video recording was explored but quickly dismissed due to the time and expertise that would be required for capturing and editing each file.

During a workshop on supporting students with dyslexia, the lecturer was introduced to the concept of Livescribe™. Further investigation revealed an electronic pen with a built-in microphone that could record both verbal and written input, storing it as interactive PDF files. This idea was integrated into the module as a series of created units covering each of the revision topics. These were accessed by 84% of a cohort of 240 students in the first trimester they were available. This positive response gave rise to a desire to bridge the gap between captured audio content and created audiovisual content. After some experimentation this was achieved using a Microsoft Surface™ tablet, enabling live annotation of visual material seen in real-time by the lecturer and students. This interactive visual content could be merged with the audio content using software such as Camtasia™, with the resulting file uploaded in mp4 format.

In order to explore student use of different media formats, podcast material was categorised as shown in figure 1.

These different types of media – captured and created; audio and audiovisual; playable online and offline – have been described collectively by Salmon et al. (2008) as *podcasts*, and the authors apply these terms collectively to the content described above. The University uses Moodle as its VLE. Moodle automatically generates and stores usage data in real-time, which gives a strong starting position from which to explore the initial proof of concept.

Created content	
Assessment video (generic)	Prepared overview of the module assessments using PowerPoint slides merged with audio commentary
Exam preparation video (generic)	Advice on how to interpret exam questions and structure answers using PowerPoint slides merged with audio commentary
Pencast	Interactive PDFs created with Livescribe™
Captured content	
Lecture (audio)	Audio capture of the weekly lecture using a voice recorder and microphone
Lecture (vodcast)	Audio capture of the weekly lecture, merged with lecture slides, annotated in real-time
Revision lecture (audio)	Audio capture of the whole revision lecture
Revision lecture (vodcast)	Audio capture of the revision lecture merged with slides, annotated in real-time
Revision segments (audio)	Audio capture of subject-specific responses to student requests for theory in revision sessions
Revision segments (vodcast)	Audio capture of subject-specific responses merged with slides, annotated in real-time

Figure 1: Podcast material categorised into different media formats.

From *accidental* to *intentional*

The Module Handbook contains a statement informing students about data collection. The statement reads as follows:

> Moodle tracks everything users do. This information is very useful in a number of ways in that it tracks the usage of specific tools but also gives a fairly accurate measure of student engagement. Your usage of the system is used as a register of engagement. The module is too big to take an accurate register in the lecture so Moodle usage is used as an electronic register. Managers require information and this is how we gather information on a very big class. If you want to see what is held then please contact the Module Leader for a copy of your tracking data.

This concept of podcasts as useful, relevant pedagogical tools has been extended beyond a single cohort to provide an accurate longitudinal picture. Data have so far been collected from seven cohorts over a 3.5-year period (that is, for every iteration of the module). It has consequently been possible to engage in two parallel reflective processes: namely, the progressive nature of the usage of these tools alongside the process of their refinement across seven cohorts. Some of these reflections have subsequently been shared with the students on the external podcast site, allowing them greater awareness of the value of capturing this information.

Data logs were first extracted from Moodle to Microsoft Excel; here, header information was removed before exportation to a database application, where some coding was required in order to group categories of data appropriately for analysis. Microsoft Access was used because its relational capabilities made it easier to link and handle data more flexibly, meaning that Moodle logs could be dynamically linked to a full list of enrolled students.

Data was then interrogated in order to explore:

1. Usage of podcasts across different media formats
2. Usage of podcasts by a single cohort over one iteration of the module
3. Pattern of podcast usage across cohorts

Do students use podcasts?

Figure 2 shows a breakdown of the data used within this research project. The material provided to each of the cohorts was not identical. As the proof of concept was established by the module leader and new technology sought, new tools were developed.

Academic Session	Cohort size	Highest use per student	Lowest use per student	Median use per student	Proportion of class using podcasts	
					Viewed any	Over 5 views
Cohort 1	273	30	0	8	99.6%	65.6%
Cohort 2	196	67	0	13	99.5%	84.7%
Cohort 3	248	61	1	13	100.0%	87.5%
Cohort 4	164	113	1	17	100.0%	91.5%
Cohort 5	204	49	1	5	100.0%	54.9%
Cohort 6	184	121	0	23	99.5%	89.1%
Cohort 7	259	159	1	27	100.0%	93.1%
All students	1528	--	--	--	99.8%	80.4%

Figure 2: Student use of podcasts by cohort.

Figure 3 shows the proportion of the cohort who used these various formats during the trimester. The results here illustrate the average value for the whole dataset of seven cohorts. It can be seen that a significant proportion of students used all of the tools that were available to them.

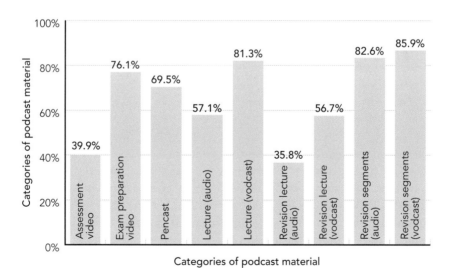

Figure 3: Student use of different categories of podcast material.

A higher proportion of students used the audiovisual material in comparison to the equivalent audio material. It is worth noting that in terms of revision material, a greater number of students used short-form podcasts (*revision segments*) instead of long-form podcasts (*revision lectures*). The pedagogical theory underpinning technology-enhanced learning tends to be focused only on designed (created) content (Mayes and de Freitas, 2013). As the data in figure 3 indicates, both captured and created podcasts were used extensively.

Having demonstrated the relevance of these tools by describing the extent of their usage, it is appropriate to explore how this varied over the period of the trimester when the module was delivered. This is illustrated in figure 4 below, again using the average value for the whole dataset of seven cohorts. *Week 0* refers to material being accessed before the start of the module.

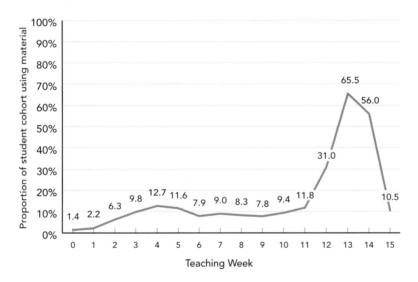

Figure 4: Proportion of students using podcasts over the duration of the module.

The data displayed here indicates that podcasts were used throughout the trimester. In fact, data not displayed on this graph indicates that podcasts in some form have been used by 99.8% of students at some point during the trimester. Podcast usage increased over the first few weeks, dipping slightly around the time of the first piece of assessment (week 5) before increasing again. It rose sharply after revision material became available, and peaked during revision week, shown here by the spike at week 13. The module exam can fall in either week 14 or week 15 of the trimester, causing the length of the module to vary.

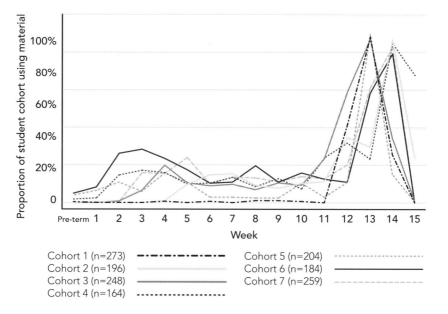

Figure 5: Proportion of students in each cohort using podcasts over the duration of the module. The total number of students across all cohorts was 1,528; the median number of students per cohort was 247.

In order to understand the impact of this in more detail, it is necessary to look at usage for each cohort represented (see figure 5). It can be seen from figure 5 that although there were variations in usage between cohorts, the overall pattern is similar. The line in figure 5 with consistently the lowest values is from the first cohort, where only audio recordings were available until week 11. The subsequent increase in usage was one of the motivators for further experimentation. The dual peaks indicate where the exam occurred in different weeks, implying that the timing of the exam affected when the material was most used. Some students continued to use the material after the exam.

The intentional podcaster: evaluation of impact

Data captured over the past seven cohorts reveal that a significant proportion of students used both captured and created tools, implying that both types of podcast are relevant. Since there is evidence that these tools were used throughout the module, they may also be considered useful. If they were not deemed as such, one would expect to see a decrease in usage as the module progressed. They were particularly well-used at revision time. The fact that podcasts can be stored and played offline means that students were able to revisit material at a time that was most useful to them, and as often as they wished. This echoes Sophie's comment that the learning taken away from attending lectures is often enhanced through listening to podcasts of those lectures. Although teachers display an understandable concern that students would be more likely to miss lectures for which a podcast was available, research indicates that this is not the case (Guertin et al., 2007; Von Konsky et al., 2009).

From the point of view of the teacher creating podcasts, it can be argued that the process is a time-efficient one, particularly with larger cohorts, since all students can access the same material at a time that suits them. Rather than spending time with many individuals on particular elements of revision, podcasts make it possible to give a higher level of support through the creation of reusable podcasts that can answer many of the students' queries. Online discussion forums can be used to deal with more specific queries not addressed by the podcast, or if further clarification is required.

As for captured podcasts, there is benefit for the teacher in opportunities for self-reflection in different areas depending on the format of the podcast. These might include elements such as content, style, pace, and degree of class engagement, and can be useful when reviewing the module for future iterations. Reflective practice is considered to be vital in the professional development of the teacher (Fry et al., 2008; Barton and Ryan, 2014).

The authors note here that none of the impacts or benefits described above are specific to the module, but rather to podcasts in general, and as such it may be argued that they are applicable to teachers working in a wide variety of subject areas.

Reflection and further developments

For each of the cohorts in the study, qualitative data have already been collected in the form of detailed questionnaires. These asked specific questions about how podcasts were used and how valuable the students found them. So far it has been possible to use the quantitative data only to establish relevance and usefulness for students, and value to the teacher. The accompanying qualitative data will provide a more complete picture of relevance, usefulness, and value.

In contrast to many studies employing questionnaire data (Saeed et al., 2009; Carvalho et al., 2009; Scutter et al., 2010; De Villiers and Walsh, 2015), these questionnaires were implemented at the end of the module, giving insight into student opinion of the podcasts they had already used (or not used), rather than indicating intention to use them. It has been shown that students' expected usage could be higher than their estimated usage (Sutton-Brady et al., 2009), so the existing data will perhaps afford a more realistic view.

When students enrol on the module they are encouraged to discover their dominant learning style at an early stage. This enables them to make the best use of the resources available to them according to their orientation towards visual, aural, reading/writing, or kinaesthetic style (in line with the recommendations of Fleming and Mills, 1992).

This information is now being collected so that the link can be explored between a student's learning style and their use of different types of podcast at different stages throughout the module. This is consistent with the position of Conole et al. (2008, p.511) who suggest that "students are immersed in a rich technology-enhanced learning environment, and they select and appropriate technologies to their own personal learning needs". The link between learning style and technology preference has been investigated in the past (for example, by Saeed et al., 2009), but the authors are not aware of any studies that involve both qualitative and quantitative data in this regard. Future analysis of the data may also consider other possible links between data characteristics, such as the student's final grade with respect to their use of podcast material during the module.

Conclusions

This chapter has demonstrated that podcasts allow a flexibility of consumption that benefits both student and tutor. The longitudinal nature of the data allows the observer to see that the majority of students exhibit strategic behaviour when accessing podcast material. It also shows that this behaviour is consistent across cohorts. Podcasts are relevant and useful to students during the revision period in particular, regardless of whether the content of the podcasts is captured or created. They have value for the tutor in terms of efficiency of time and consistency of support that may not otherwise be possible for a large cohort, plus they enable a high degree of reflective practice: an important contributor to professional development.

The authors encourage the reader to find their own starting point and explore the concept for their own practice. First steps may involve investigating what equipment or software is available, either at individual or institutional level, or finding a local champion. Those who already use podcasts will hopefully agree that podcasting need not be a complex or costly exercise, and will be encouraged to develop their teaching into new areas.

Stephen Robertson is a lecturer in Business Management at Edinburgh Napier University. He joined the University in 2008 after the completion of his MBA. Prior to this, Stephen spent almost 20 years in the IT industry during which he led a wide range of project and support teams. This broad experience underpins his creation of a learning environment that extends beyond the classroom using a range of social media to encourage student engagement. Other research interests include the Business of Professional Football in Scotland and cross-cultural interprofessional ethical practice. In his free time, Stephen manages the successful University Football 1st XI.

Sarah Sholl joined Edinburgh Napier University in 2015, following a Post-Doctoral Research Fellowship at the University of Dundee. She previously held a management role for eight years at the Royal College of Surgeons of Edinburgh, and prior to that was a researcher in forensic medicine at the University of Glasgow. Sarah lectures at undergraduate and postgraduate level in strategic management and research skills, and is Module Leader for Contemporary Issues in Strategic Management. In addition to a growing interest in the development and use of pedagogical tools, Sarah's other research interests include cultures influencing workplace learning, inter-professional team learning, and the balance of service delivery and training in healthcare management.

Notes

1. Her real name, used with her permission and encouragement.

References

Barton, G. and Ryan, M. (2014). Multimodal approaches to reflective teaching and assessment in higher education. *Higher Education Research and Development*, 33 (3), 409–424.

Carvalho, A. A., Aguiar, C., Santos, H., Oliveira, L., Marques, A. and Maciel, R. (2009). Podcasts in higher education: students' and lecturers' perspectives. In: Tatnall, A. and Jones. A., (Eds.). *Education and Technology for a Better World*. Springer: Berlin, Heidelberg, 417–426.

Conole, G., de Laat, M., Dillon, T., and Darby, J. (2008). "Disruptive technologies", "pedagogical innovation": what's new? Findings from an in-depth study of students' use and perception of technology. *Computers and Education*, 50 (2), 511–524.

Danielson, J., Preast, V., Bender, H. and Hassall, L. (2014). Is the effectiveness of lecture capture related to teaching approach or content type? *Computers and Education*, 72, 121–131.

De Villiers, M. and Walsh, S. (2015). How podcasts influence medical students' learning – a descriptive qualitative study. *African Journal of Health Professions Education*, 7 (1), 130–133.

Evans, C. (2008). The effectiveness of m-learning in the form of podcast revision lectures in higher education. *Computers and Education*, 50 (2), 491–498.

Fleming, N.D. and Mills, C. (1992). Not another inventory, rather a catalyst for reflection. *To Improve the Academy*, 11, 137–155. University of Nebraska.

Fry, H., Ketteridge, S. and Marshall, S. (2008). *A Handbook for Teaching and Learning in Higher Education: Enhancing Academic Practice*. Abingdon: Routledge.

Guertin, L. A., Bodek, M. J., Zappe, S. E. and Kim, H. (2007). Questioning the student use of and desire for lecture podcasts. *MERLOT Journal of Online Learning and Teaching*, 3 (2), 133–141.

Hammersley, B. (2004). Audible revolution. *The Guardian*. [Online]. Available at: http://www.theguardian.com/media/2004/feb/12/broadcasting.digitalmedia [Accessed 12 February 2016].

Lonn, S. and Teasley, S. (2009). Podcasting in higher education: what are the implications for teaching and learning? *Internet and Higher Education*, 12 (2), 88–92.

Margaryan, A., Littlejohn, A. and Vojt, G. (2011). Are digital natives a myth or reality? University students' use of digital technologies. *Computers and Education*, 56 (2), 429–440.

Mayes, T. and de Freitas, S. (2013). Technology-enhanced learning: the role of theory. In: Beetham, H. and Sharpe, R. (Eds.). *Rethinking Pedagogy for a Digital Age*. 2nd Edition, New York: Routledge, 17–30.

Saeed, N., Yang, Y. and Sinnappan, S. (2009). Emerging web technologies in higher education: a case of incorporating blogs, podcasts and social bookmarks in a web programming course based on students' learning styles and technology preferences. *Journal of Educational Technology and Society*, 12 (4), 98–109.

Salmon, G. and Edirisingha, P. (2008) (Eds.). *Podcasting for Learning in Universities*. Maidenhead, England: Open University Press.

Scutter, S., Stupans, I., Sawyer, T. and King, S. (2010). How do students use podcasts to support learning? *Australasian Journal of Educational Technology*, 26 (2), 180–191.

Sutton-Brady, C., Scott, K. M., Taylor, L., Carabetta, G. and Clark, S. (2009). The value of using short-format podcasts to enhance learning and teaching. *Research in Learning Technology*, 17 (3), 219–232.

Von Konsky, B. R., Ivins, J. and Gribble, S. J. (2009). Lecture attendance and web-based lecture technologies: a comparison of student perceptions and usage patterns. *Australasian Journal of Educational Technology*, 25 (4), 581–595.

The ascendency of digital discourse: a reflection on two informal collaborative online learning interactions – Twitter and the Social Gathering

Laurence Patterson

ABSTRACT

The MSc programme under consideration is an award-winning, work-based qualification that attracts an international student body of practitioners. It draws from those supporting learning, teaching, and assessment within Higher Education and Further Education, from schools, and from the private sector. The programme offers grounding in the constructive pedagogic principles behind appropriate online learning and teaching, providing students space to reflect on and make changes to their own education practice, through use of technology. The social constructivist theory of knowledge most accurately reflects the practice engaged in by the programme's academic team.

This chapter explores the development of mediated, weekly Twitter sessions that offer cohorts an opportunity to engage in a lighter way across each of the seven modules of study which make up the programme. The sessions offer discourse relevant to themes in units of study and a chance for students to talk openly about their development. The chapter looks, too, at an informal online gathering of students and alumni, alongside current and previous programme academics in synchronous online discussion through a tool called WebEX – motivating the students to engage in a series of collaborative activities.

Finally, the chapter attempts to map these developments to the Community of Inquiry framework, offering considerations for readers wishing to engage in similar activities with their students.

Keywords: digital, discourse, eLearning, Community of Inquiry framework

Introduction

Reflective abstraction is grounded in the actions not of the individual, the developmental psychologist Jean Piaget (2001) tells us, but in the actions of the many. From Piaget, a logical move might take us across to the work of Vygotsky (1962), who tells us that social interactions are the very catalyst for cognitive development, and that these found the beginnings of a social constructivist approach to learning and teaching.

The social constructivist approach is one that has defined much of curriculum design and delivery in western universities over the last 30 years (Selwyn, 2011), and has run roughly in tandem with ubiquity of access to learning technologies. The architecture of modern western universities is likely to be sympathetic to the approach, with physical classroom and library spaces designed to accommodate a wide range of dialogic and group-based activities. In questioning what a modern-day Vygotskian classroom may look like, Maddux, LaMont Johnson and Willis (2001) suggest that a curriculum design and learning environment enriched by interventions that improve social and collaborative activity are key. In their digital spaces, universities also seek to construct knowledge through a variety of designs and approaches, augmented by software motivating discussion and reflection; Selwyn, too, says that "technology is seen as a key means of facilitating a learner's exploration and construction of knowledge" (2011, p.74).

This chapter reflects on the development of two technology interventions adopted to support students on a Master's programme of study in a Scottish Higher Education institution. In doing so it seems to informally map the inventions across Garrison, Anderson and Archer's (2001) respected Community of Inquiry framework, and to provide lessons learned for continuing learning and teaching practice of the programme. Further on, the chapter discusses the contribution that such interactions may make towards modelling good educational practice for its students.

The MSc programme was a double award-winner at the eAssessment Scotland 2012 Awards. It is an online programme which attracts an international student body of practitioners and those supporting learning, teaching and assessment within HE, FE, schools, and the private sector. Up to 60 students across three or four cohorts engage with core educational principles and theories, with materials and with each other, toward an authentic grounding in constructive pedagogic principles behind appropriate online learning and teaching. They augment their own practice through contrasting technologies, and reflect and evaluate impact. The full MSc is studied over seven 20-credit, 15-week modules, each of which explores contemporary themes related to the overall programme. It has its own set of learning outcomes, assessment criteria, reading lists, and module leader. Each module is, in turn, made up of around four or five units of delivery shaping a formative path to the final summative assessment. Units tend to take a focused approach to an aspect of the module, through the requirement for students to complete a given activity or engage in a themed discussion. A 40-credit dissertation module, undertaken in the final stages of the programme, takes a more self-directed approach and includes supervisory support from an academic member of staff.

For students on the MSc, knowledge is constructed not only within the given learning environment and through the formal mechanisms for engagement, but across a range of non-formal and informal sources (Eraut, 2000). Implicitly, from the first module until the last, the programme promotes a culture of sharing and engagement across a social group. Each of the modules seeks to stimulate interaction and discussion of relevant themes across online forums; they also provide forums for engagement in outside areas. In an early example of the programme, students collaborate to create and facilitate a two-week online seminar. One of the objectives of the MSc is to observe and project good practice in the use of contemporary technologies for education; a further objective is to communicate, authentically, what it is like to be an online student.

The Community of Inquiry (CoI) model

In building their knowledge on the principles of blended and online education, the students of the MSc programme observed here engage in an understanding of and reflection on Garrison, Anderson and Archer's (2001) Community of Inquiry (CoI) model (see figure 1, overleaf), described by its authors as follows: "an educational community of inquiry is a group of individuals who collaboratively engage in purposeful critical discourse and reflection to construct personal meaning and confirm mutual understanding" (2011, p.15). The model indicates the interdependence of three key elements, which together may create a meaningful learning experience: the social, cognitive, and teaching presences.

The CoI model presents three principle elements for a successful educational experience: social presence, cognitive presence, and teaching presence. A social presence might best be described as the formally constructed environment for engagement – the location, room or forum. A cognitive presence is less easy to define, but concerns the academic discourse from which the construction of meaning might occur. Finally, a teaching presence may be observed as the facilitation of the two other processes to achieve understanding and comprehension. The model has served well as a framework for plotting and observing experience across entire programmes of study (APUS, 2016), as well as in individual activities; for example, in the use of Second Life (Burgess et al., 2009) and reflective blogs (Yang, 2009).

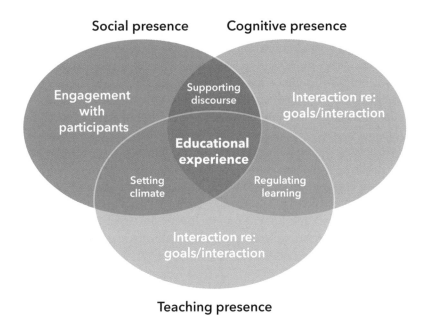

Figure 1: The Community of Inquiry framework (image under CC licence (CC-BY-SA 3.0)).

The CoI is purposefully modelled within the MSc programme; the chapter refers to it when considering the impact on learning of the two interactions discussed here. When looking at formal activities (for example, in the designed online discussions of the first module in the MSc), a social presence is observed in the Moodle course and the educational forums themselves, a cognitive presence in the located interactions within the forum environment. A teaching presence can be suggested in the directing role of the module leader, who should steer discussions in an appropriate area. Forum activities, then, can be seen to be well-centred and are at the intersection of all three presences in the CoI framework, although adaptive to the requirements of the cohort (for example, the need for a stronger teacher presence at the module start). In Module Two of the MSc, student groups begin to co-design and deliver a two-week seminar to the remainder of the cohort in an area broadly of their choosing, but within the frame of the unit in question. Moodle, the Virtual Learning Environment (VLE), offers a formal social presence, but students are encouraged to (and often do) choose to engage together in groups across non-formal environments such as Skype and email. For their group-led seminar delivery Moodle affords a likely cognitive presence, but groups may choose a different platform to engage with their learners. Clearly the teacher presence in this example is not the formal module leader, despite their overall moderation of activities, but the group itself. Arguably plotted to the centre of the CoI module this activity shifts our understanding of what a non-traditional community of inquiry may look like.

A central rationale for the development of both Twitter and the Social Gathering in the programme is located in the belief that learning does indeed occur through constructed opportunities, which explore scenarios and themes in informal ways – during which collaboration and engagement is spontaneous – that may support the core learning activities of modules. Interactions are intended to extend the community of practice's dialogue beyond the construct of the dedicated online environment (VLE), affording opportunities to engage between cohorts and with individuals outside of the programme altogether.

Ethical approval has been sought by the author of this chapter from all current students on the MSc programme and from current programme academic colleagues. Some names, Twitter handles, programme and course names have been omitted.

Reflecting on Twitter

Riazat (2013) suggests that we have entered a third wave in our understanding of digital discourse. First and second web technologies familiar to researchers, academics, and students – electronic mailing lists and reflective blogs – are now in decline. The author asserts that it remains for micro-blogging and semi-synchronous online activities to take an significant place in debate and dialogue.

Introducing Twitter to the programme

The @BOEBuzz Twitter account was created to communicate programme news and announcements, and was also used to report and retweet stories relevant to technology and education. Engagement between tutors, students, and MSc students across Twitter was rare. @BOEBuzz continues to be used by the programme team today but, as we shall see, its focus is towards collaboration.

The opportunities for dialogue sit at the heart of Twitter. Within it, the hashtag allows for dialogue on a specific theme to be brought together by adding the symbol to the body of a tweet. For example, a tweet with the hashtag #thursday will appear in a list resulting from a search made on Twitter for *Thursday*. Four years after @BOEBuzz was established, academic colleagues on the programme considered how Twitter's hashtag might be used to motivate dialogue between cohorts of students. The resulting project, #EDNA, took its lead from the now well-established #PhDchat discussion. #PhDchat is a community that brings together tweets from doctoral students, researchers, and supervisors to an audience of well over half a million. As any conference attendee will know, adding a *#name* to a tweet will expose it on a list with that name. #PhDchat is unrestricted – not owned or moderated by any one individual (arguably except Twitter) – but open and accessible to all, with a Wednesday evening-focused live chat.

The programme team created three Twitter hashtags and promoted them to students across three separate postgraduate programmes of study. A charter of etiquette and "getting started with Twitter" guides were created and shared across cohorts. Taking the lead from #PhDchat, a live chat time was proposed for each week of the trimester to bring focus to the free-flowing tweeted conversations anticipated through the remainder of the week. A new Twitter account was created with the name @EDNAProject, to centrally manage all tweets created by the programme teams.

Developing Tweet-Ups

The first #EDNA Tweet-Up was facilitated by colleagues from one of the programmes during a January evening. A handful of students joined the discussion and engaged a little, but successive weeks saw fewer attending, despite reminders. One month later, the first #EDNA session was run by a second programme. Only one student joined the discussion; again, further weeks attracted few, if any. Through the course of the summer break those students who had not participated in Twitter sessions were asked why. Some felt fear in their thoughts being exposed across a public forum; others commented that they felt uncomfortable using a social tool such as Twitter for educational purposes.

Tweet-Ups began on the MSc programme for the first time in September of that year, with a cohort of students beginning their studies with the first module. The academic team aimed to normalise, as much as was possible, the ongoing discourse in Twitter and the weekly live sessions. Signposts were added to welcome messages, posted by the module leader each Monday within the VLE. A schedule of live sessions was created and published. Crucially, the module leader engaged with students on Twitter by creating a list of current students' accounts, retweeting their relevant tweets, and including them in newly produced messages. Of an initial cohort of 25, the first MSc live Tweet-Up attracted interactions from 17. Successive live sessions lost a number of students but retained a good flow, with discussions moving between themes discussed in the module, and more random and humorous dialogue. This cohort was highly engaged in Twitter outside of the live sessions, too, often tweeting a relevant news item or comment about life as an online learner – tagging in @BOEBuzz, #EDNABOE, or the programme staff directly.

Reflecting on the Social Gathering

As part of their standard delivery model, module leaders on the programme use WebEX, web-based virtual conference software supplied by the University. This offers a synchronous environment and weekly one-hour engagements with students, and affords a number of elements familiar to those engaging with similar software: audio and video streaming, an interactive digital whiteboard, a polling system, screen, and application sharing are all standard. Activity can be recorded and the hour-long session made available to listen to at a later time. Typically, module leaders will guide the dialogue towards the themes presented in the module that week and offer formative guidance towards assessment.

Introducing the Social Gathering to the programme

Plans for extending the use of WebEX had been discussed by the programme team around the same time as the first #EDNA Tweet-Ups, with a view to complementing current practice with an informal online Social Gathering *across* cohorts. The ideas were motivated, in the first instance, by the desire to communicate to all cohorts the changes that the MSc had undergone. The makeup of the programme team itself was almost entirely new, and it was considered that such an event would introduce them to the cohort of students. In addition, two modules had been redesigned by the team and two others had been replaced, to be taught for the first time from September.

The first online Social Gathering took place in June of that year and was facilitated through WebEX; there were no more than 15 people attending, with at least four from each MSc cohort. Invitations were sent to all current students, to alumni of the programme, and to current and previous MSc academic staff. The mood of the Gathering was decidedly lighter and more open than that of the weekly Virtual Office Hours (VOH) sessions; familiar elements of WebEX were exploited, however, in that the Gathering was guided by the programme leader. Through the course of the hour, communication occurred in two channels: through the text chat-based stream and verbally. Attendees were invited to "lift their mic" when they wished to comment. This basic accepted *netiquette* was familiar from past attendances of the VOHs.

At the start of the Gathering all attendees' access was raised to *presenter*, allowing them to annotate content placed on the whiteboard. An image of the map of the world was placed there, with each attendee asked to mark, using an arrow, where they were speaking from. As an ice-breaker, this activity succeeded in bringing focus to the central discussions. Some time was taken for all to introduce themselves before conversation turned to the changes in the MSc. On reflection, the first Gathering offered little opportunity for verbal discourse, as the programme leader guided much of the discussion. But engagement in the chat room was strong and, at times, comments and questions became the focus.

In the days after the Gathering the MSc students had said that they enjoyed many aspects of the evening: the opportunity to meet and find out more about others further on or a little further back in the programme, the lighter feel to the discussion, and the sense that what was said might not have been evaluated and judged to the degree that it might be during the VOHs.

A central theme of one of the new MSc modules, to be delivered to Diploma-level students in January, was the role that play takes in learning: establishing the importance of simulation, fun, and games to human cognitive development. Activities garnering play would be the driving force behind the second Gathering (see figure 2), which took a more informal approach when it was run just before the start of the Christmas Holidays. Around the same number of students and academic colleagues attended, and WebEX was, again, the collaboration tool used.

Developing the Social Gathering

From the outset, those attending had been told that they were split into two teams, with each led by programme academics. Prior to the Gathering those academics had been given sealed envelopes and told not to open them until a specific point in the hour.

Once more, a world map was placed on the WebEX whiteboard and, this time, attendees were invited to mark where they were born. A person from

Split into Groups

1 Welcome – a bit like an hour of your favourite quiz (2 minutes)

2 Birth map – where you were born on a map (2 minutes)

3 Introductions – with a twist: two truths and a lie (10 minutes)

4 Choose your team names – two minutes to consider and relay back the reason for the name (3 minutes)

5 Picture scavenger hunt (10 minutes)

6 One minute please (10 minutes)

7 Questions – Pub quiz: fifteen questions (18 minutes)

- What is Tiger Woods' first name? (Eldrick)
- Which actress starred in *High Society*? (Grace Kelly)
- Which 60s rock group recorded *Whiter Shade of Pale*? (Procol Harum)
- How many men have walked on the moon: 4, 8, or 12? (12)
- Which is the world's second largest country in land area? (Canada)
- What is the most common blood type in humans? (Type O)
- The name of which area in the Pacific means "many islands"? (Polynesia)
- There are only four words in the English language which end in *–dous*. Two are *tremendous* and *stupendous*. Name the other two. (*Horrendous* and *hazardous*)
- What is the currency of Switzerland? (Swiss Franc)
- Which is the largest planet in the solar system? (Jupiter)
- What is triskadekaphobia? (Fear of the number 13)
- One tablespoon equals how many teaspoons? (3)
- What is the capital of the Netherlands? (The Hague)
- In which country was Mel Gibson born? (US [not Australia])
- What is the Mexican food gazpacho? (Cold soup)
- Name ALL of the seven dwarves. (Bashful, Doc, Dopey, Grumpy, Happy, Sleepy, Sneezy)
- In the carol *Twelve Days of Christmas*, what is the total number of gifts that *my true love gave to me*? (364)
- Gerontology is the study of what? (Old age, elderly, the aged, etc.)
- How is the year 1999 written in roman numerals? (MCMXCIX)

8 Answers and winner

Figure 2: Facilitator's run-through of the second Social Gathering.

each team was then invited to offer two truths and a lie about themselves, which the other team had to identify. Team leaders were asked to open their envelopes, and found that they contained a written list of items which teams were required to find across the Internet and deliver in an email to the programme leader before the hour was complete. A number from each team continued to engage with the treasure hunt, whilst others took part in a kind of pub quiz, verbally answering questions set by the facilitator. Points were allocated for a correct answer and deducted for a wrong one. Scores from the quiz were added to correctly-discovered treasure hunt items, one of the teams was declared the winner, and the activities of the Gathering were complete.

Discussion of the outcomes and contribution to academic practice

Almost exactly one year after the first #EDNA Tweet-Up, the @EDNAProject account and #EDNABOE hashtag were superseded by a return to @BOEBuzz, which became the direct line for dialogue across Twitter. Students appeared to prefer tweets that did not need the #EDNABOE hashtag, something they often failed to remember to add. An unexpected outcome of using Twitter on the MSc was that discussions were joined by people from outside the cohort (see figure 3).

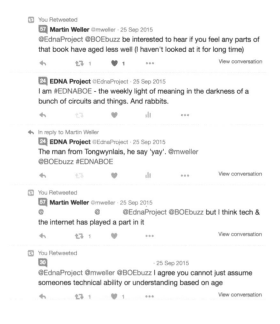

Figure 3: Twitter conversation
between the programme students and
Martin Weller (author of core text).

At the outset, this chapter touched on the workings of the constructivist approach to learning and teaching. Through the thoughts of Piaget (2001) and Vygotsky (1962), an understanding of the movement towards socially constructed knowledge has developed, stimulating an architectural change that places the teacher in the facilitating and guiding role. Students of the first module were required to learn about this approach, and to engage from the beginning of their studies with the reading of Selwyn (2011), Weller (2003), and Littlejohn and Pegler (2007). Their immersion in the work of these authors would allow them to understand a range of pedagogic approaches ranging from behaviourism to constructivism, and the beginnings of curriculum and assessment design for online and blended delivery. Students were pleased to be able to ask those authors directly about their work through the course of their Twitter activities. Martin Weller joined the group to talk about his popular *Myths of eLearning*. Sessions were also joined by JISC, who discussed Augmented Reality in Education, and organisations such as The Ragged University and DigitalMe, in conversation about Digital Badges.

Reflections on Twitter and the Social Gathering

Generally, MSc students introduced to @BOEBuzz from Module Two and beyond did not interact with it. However, those in the most recent cohort (whose starting point was with their first module) continued to engage voluntarily. Many students who took part in the facilitated weekly sessions were later using Twitter independently of the module leader, engaging with each other as they moved through the second module. This informal discourse is now more popular than the focused hourly meetings, which originally started the development.

The approach taken in facilitating the first Social Gathering (see figure 4, overleaf) shared much in common with that of traditional weekly collaborations on the programme. The WebEX environment, with its set of tools, was familiar to those that had attended VOHs; there was a presumed etiquette and pattern of behaviour, shared by both interactions: introductions, opportunities for group discussion on a topic, and the presence of a programme academic. The theme of the second Gathering, although not connected with the programme curriculum and motivated by play, was more directed, with fewer opportunities for discourse engagement. The first covered more formal issues in a less formalised way; the second was constructed more formally but covered less formal themes. In the days after the event, students said that they very much enjoyed the hour but felt that the need to work across a number of games was exhausting.

The development of the MSc Twitter presence, Tweet-Ups and Social Gatherings were intended to map onto the balanced central spot in the Community of Inquiry framework, offering mediated discourse and dialogue through weekly focused sessions and periodic late-evening WebEX sessions. Both were to dovetail with weekly VOH sessions, which bring students together to discuss module activities; these are mediated by the module leader, and therefore take a semi-formal approach. A cognitive presence would be felt in Tweet-Ups through a weekly advertised schedule of themes to be discussed in Social Gatherings through a plan of content akin to a lesson plan. A social presence would occur through the multimodal means of communication in both developments and a teaching presence would be seen in the organised and facilitated nature of the developments.

Figure 4: Twitter reaction, the morning after the second Twitter Gathering.

In reality, @BOEBuzz may be seen to be located at the intersection between social and cognitive presence in the framework (see figure 1) named *supporting discourse*. Contrary to the view expressed by some (Annand, 2011), who question the extent to which a social presence contributes to discourse and knowledge construction, the programme's students were found to engage in meaningful discussions more fully *away* from the weekly Tweet-Ups, necessarily without any type of formal teaching presence. Garrison, Anderson and Archer (2001) may argue that the apparently missing presence is in fact alive and well, but is activated, informally, within the constructive frame afforded by Twitter itself. It is certainly true that, although Tweet-Ups engaged and offered opportunities for discourse, fewer students exploited this opportunity. Clearly Twitter was not a tool affording equal engagement for all cohorts; it was apparent that those introduced to it from the beginning would be more likely to embed it into their own professional practices.

The Social Gathering is likely to map more closely towards the intersection between social and teaching presence in the CoI framework (see figure 1) named *setting climate*: intending an opportunity for engagement outside of the themes of the programme, but requiring the facilitation by one of the programme's academic staff. The Gathering works well when framed as an end-of-academic-year event without a specific agenda. Students are relatively passive, with limited opportunities for discourse and engagement. This arguably contrasts with weekly Virtual Office Hour sessions, whose focus is formal and tends towards the delivered curriculum, their place mapping more effectively to the centre of Garrison, Anderson and Archer's (2001) framework.

Each of the three intersections of the CoI, shown in figure 6 (*supporting discourse, regulating learning,* and *setting climate*) represent valid and constructive curriculum design outcomes. The mapping done by this chapter suggests that the programme's use of Twitter has been an effective catalyst in supporting discourse across a limited range of cohorts, whilst its use of the Social Gathering has created and supported the culture of online learning and collaboration. For balance, it might be observed that instances of regulating learning – the intersection between *cognitive presence* and *teaching presence* – exist along the design of the programme, from the construct of the VLE itself to self and peer assessment opportunities.

Conclusion and possible future developments

With the principal understanding that the construction of learning around a community of inquiry is a positive thing (Levine, 2010), further development of Twitter and the Social Gathering as informal communities on the MSc programme will continue. Annand (2011) and Xin (2012) critique the CoI framework and, in particular, the social presence aspect of it – believing that the construction of meaningful knowledge can and does occur in the absence of formal processes of engagement. Xin tells us that online expressions may be seen as inherently social. Despite the location of both developments away from the centre of the CoI framework, the team members continue to see the importance of informal routes to digital discourse for their students.

It is recognised that these are early days in exploring how Twitter and the Social Gathering may support learning. The success of informal interactions depends on the buy-in of students. In the case of Twitter, discourse has continued away from weekly focused and facilitated Tweet-Ups and some students have engaged with it. Tweet-Ups themselves have tended to attract only those introduced to Twitter on the programme from the beginning, and only two of the four academic colleagues have engaged. If future cohorts are to take part, it is important for the programme to agree upon a direction and to introduce that from the first week of study. A third online Social Gathering is planned; the academic team recognise WebEX as the most appropriate tool, and will continue the fun, informal approach. The MSc programme's academic team has gained confidence in handling the event, and in preparing a variety of possible activities they hope to explore.

Garrison and Anderson (2011) tell us that a Community of Inquiry "represents a process of creating a deep and meaningful (collaborative-constructivist) learning experience through the development of three interdependent elements – social, cognitive and teaching presence" (ibid, p.15). In its drive to support a meaningful learning experience, this MSc offers consideration towards the breadth of opportunities for engagement with digital discourse.

Meaningful discourse is likely to emerge outside of facilitated Tweet-Ups with a larger number of students; some work will still be required to engage them in Twitter and through Social Gatherings further into their studies. Opportunities may exist to expand numbers by widening participation, perhaps by connecting with students in similar programmes across the world.

Considerations for adoption

The following brief suggestions may offer guidance for academic staff wishing to explore the development of a Twitter presence or Social Gathering.

1. Establish a baseline for required student engagement from the start. Define the learner and teacher requirements, the chosen platform, frequency, and scope.
2. Discuss whether developments are entirely informal, formal, or with elements of both. To what degree will they offer supplementary support to the learning on the course?
3. If using Twitter: might students wish to sign up with a new account, rather than use an existing one? Consider making available good practice guidelines from the start.

4. Is attendance compulsory? Can students be assessed against their attendance? Can module Learning Outcomes be plotted to developments?
5. Where on the CoI framework do you wish for your developments to be plotted? Why? How will you get there? How will you measure achievement?

The author of this chapter is grateful to colleagues from Edinburgh Napier University for their support in creating #EDNA.

Laurence Patterson has worked in Higher Education since 1998, and at Edinburgh Napier University since 2005 – initially as the institution's eLearning Adviser, and more recently as programme leader for the MSc Blended and Online Education. His interests lie around digital practice and online curriculum design, as well as in emerging technologies and digital literacies. Laurence is a Senior Fellow of the Higher Education Academy and a member of Edinburgh Napier's Teaching Fellow community. He begins his PhD studies on academic publishing in September 2016.

References

Annand, D. (2011). Social Presence within the Community of Inquiry framework. *The International Review of Research in Open and Distributed Learning*, 12 (5) [Online]. Available at: http://www.irrodl.org/index.php/irrodl/article/view/924/1855 [Accessed 13 March 2016].

APUS (2016). The Community of Inquiry [Online]. Available at: http://www.apus.edu/ctl/faculty/community-of-inquiry [Accessed 13 March 2016].

Burgess, M. L., Slate, J. R., Rojas-LeBouef, A. and LaPrairie, K. (2009). Teaching and learning in Second Life: using the Community of Inquiry (CoI) model to support online instruction with graduate students in instructional technology. *Internet and Higher Education*, 13 (1), 84–88.

Eraut, M. (2000). Non-formal learning and tacit knowledge in professional work. *British Journal of Educational Psychology*, 70 (1), 113–136.

Garrison, D. R., Anderson, T. and Archer, W. (2001). Critical thinking, cognitive presence and computer conferencing in distance education. *American Journal of Distance Education*, 15 (1), 7–23.

Garrison, D. R. and Anderson, T. (2011). *E-Learning in the 21ˢᵗ Century: A Framework for Research and Practice*. London: Routledge Falmer.

Levine, T. H. (2010). Tools for the study and design of collaborative teacher learning: the affordances of different conceptions of teacher community and activity theory. *Teacher Education Quarterly*, 37 (1), 109–130.

Littlejohn, A. and Pegler, C. (2007). *Preparing for Blended E-Learning*. London: Routledge.

Maddux, C. D., LaMont Johnson, D. and Willis, J. W. (2001). *Educational Computing: Learning with Tomorrow's Technologies*. 3rd edn. Pearson.

Piaget, J. (2001). *The Language and Thought of the Child*. London: Routledge.

Riazat, N. (2013). #PhDchat – a doctoral and academic research community [Online]. Available at: http://www.phd2published.com/2013/03/21/phdchat-a-doctoral-and-academic-research-community-by-nasima-riazat/ [Accessed 12 February 2016].

Selwyn, N. (2011). *Education and Technology: Key Issues and Debates*. London: Continuum.

Vygotsky, L. S. (1962). *Thought and Language*. Cambridge MA: MIT Press.

Weller, M. (2003). *Delivering Learning on the Net: The Why, What and How of Online Education*. London: Routledge Falmer.

Yang, S. (2009). Using blogs to enhance critical reflection and community of practice. *Journal of Educational Technology and Society*, 12 (2), 11–21.

Every picture tells a story: using selfie-inspired activities to enhance social relations and encourage self-reflexivity

Mabel Victoria

ABSTRACT

This chapter explores the results of a study in Thailand that capitalised on the popularity of the selfie, providing second-year English language students with an opportunity to practise their oral presentation and speaking skills. The selfie was used not in the usual sense of online picture-sharing, but as a visual aid in a face-to-face interaction. Mining the rich insights gained from the Thai study, this chapter presents another selfie-inspired activity adapted for a different context and purpose at a UK university. Initially designed to facilitate recall of students' names linked with faces, the initiative evolved into an effective conversation starter. It is suggested that both selfie-inspired initiatives have led to serendipitous results, such as encouraging self-reflexivity among the students and promoting the development of "rapid intimacy" in the classroom. Indeed, creating a space for students to share their personal stories and enact different identities can help enrich the learning and teaching experience. This chapter also demonstrates how aspects of visual methodologies can be employed as a resource for theorising visual data, such as the selfie, for classroom application.

Introduction

The selfie, a modern version of the self-portrait, is usually taken with a hand-held device and intended for sharing online via social networking media; it has become the subject of much discussion and debate in the past few years. The opposing camps consist of the *haters* and the *likers*, with the practice of taking one's picture and posting it online for all the digital world to see being both "adored and reviled" (Murray, 2015, p.490). Those who revile the selfie view it as an "expression of narcissism gone wild" (Giroux, 2015, p.163), a sign of pathology including psychosis and body image disorder (Senft and Baym, 2015), a "visual expression of vanity" (Murray, 2015, p.499) representative of "profound loneliness" (ibid, p.491), a "sad form of exhibitionism" (Wortham, 2013, p.4), and "an indication of the public's descent into the narrow orbits of self-obsession" (Giroux, 2015, p.158). While mindful of these negative associations regarding the selfie, its pervasive influence as a global phenomenon, especially among young people, cannot be ignored (Senft and Baym, 2015). Dismissing it as mere manifestations of a vain and narcissistic culture may lead us to overlook its potential pedagogical application in light of the fact that the practice is quite prevalent among college students (Katz and Crocker, 2015).

The selfie is considered by some scholars as a powerful "outlet for self-definition" (Murray, 2015, p.2) and self-expression (Iqani and Schroeder, 2015). It can also be viewed as a medium for identity formation, self-presentation and sociality (Gye, 2007), and personal reflexivity (Frosh, 2015). Taking into consideration possible pitfalls and potential surrounding the selfie, the initiatives reported in this chapter were designed to capitalise on the interests of the students, most of whom can be seen as "adorers" of the selfie phenomenon (Murray, 2015). This chapter is an exploration into how the notion of the selfie was used as an inspiration to serve pedagogical outcomes. It should be noted that a selfie, as deployed in this research, does not only mean one face or one person, but also includes other variations such as a group selfie and text-based material with photographs.

Description of the selfie initiative: Thai university context

This initiative was conducted while working in Thailand as a Teacher of English as a Foreign Language (TEFL) in 2014. The students who took part were taking a course called *Effective Communication*, the main aim of which was to help students improve their listening and oral communication skills. It was felt that the selfie-inspired activity was an appropriate exercise that would enable the students to talk about a topic that they knew better than anybody else: themselves. In brief, the activity entailed that the students take selfies during a two-week period. They then had to select one selfie as a talking point for a ten-minute oral presentation in class.

The class consisted of 28 English language learners; 5 males and 23 females, between 19 and 22 years old, all second-year students. Their level of English was between intermediate to upper intermediate, indicating an ability to use English with a certain degree of fluency. All the students in the class had smartphones, which they used to take pictures of lecture slides, text on the whiteboard, their classmates' notes, or pages from a book. Sometimes they even tried to take selfies discreetly while doing group work, or when there were transitions between activities. Following Zinn and Scheuer (2006) and their notion of a good teacher, the selfie-inspired project was conceptualised in order to exploit the students' existing interests with the goal of helping them practise their English language fluency. The notion of fluency is conceptualised here as the learner's focus on the communication of message or content rather than being inhibited by concentrating on the grammatical correctness of an utterance. In other words, it is believed that when language learners are motivated to communicate a particular message, they are then able to "integrate previously encountered language items into an easily accessed, largely unconscious, language system" (Nation, 1989, p.378).

As mentioned earlier, the students were asked to take selfies over a two-week period during the semester break. Alternatively, it was suggested that they could also select from any of their favourite selfies taken previously. They then chose a particular selfie to present in class by way of a slide presentation. To prepare for their talk, the students were given a set of reflective questions to think about. The guide questions asked the student when and where was the selfie taken, what they were doing before and after the picture was taken, and if they were alone or with other people. They were also asked how they would describe themselves – their appearance, feelings, and state of mind when the selfie was taken. In what way did the image represent who they really are? Why did they choose this particular selfie to present to the class?

Before the presentations, the students were given the opportunity to practise their talk in small groups to work on their pronunciation and fluency. It also provided them with a comfortable space so that they might feel more confident before their talk in front of the whole class. With the anticipation that it might be intimidating for some students, they were assured that it was entirely up to each individual to decide what they wished to share about themselves. At the end of each presentation, the listeners were encouraged to ask questions or offer comments.

After all 28 presentations, which took place over a period of two and a half weeks[1], the students were asked what they thought about the selfie initiative. They indicated that they enjoyed talking about their selfies, which can be considered a "happy side-effect" (Gauntlett and Holzwarth 2006, p.82). It is of course acknowledged that due to the asymmetrical power relations in class, students were not likely to voice out negative feelings about the activity. However, based on observation during the selfie presentations, the students appeared very engaged and animated. There was also a robust discussion about the selfie – both its positive and negative aspects – and how it had been used on social media platforms such as Facebook. The de-briefing provided an opportunity for the students to touch upon related issues such as social media and body image, and the relationship between self-esteem and the number of "likes" on Facebook. The extended discussion on the selfie and social media platforms, although unplanned, was encouraged. It demonstrated that the task generated authentic language use.

Method

It should be clarified that the selfie project described above was designed and implemented as a regular speaking activity, and not as a formal research undertaking. However, motivated by an innate researcher mentality not to let a set of very rich, serendipitous data to slip by, it was decided to evolve the activity into a more formal study. Indeed, it has been argued that surprising findings and fortuitous circumstances are legitimate reasons for carrying out research (Hammersley and Atkinson, 2007). This is also in line with ethnographic principles and the use of naturally occurring data. In this particular case, the pre-collected data consisted of the selfies and observation notes during the presentations.

The decision to make the activity an opportunistic research undertaking was discussed with the students after the presentations had taken place. Once approval was gained from the ethics committee of the university, the students were asked if they would give their written consent for the observation notes and digital selfies to be used as part of the data set. It was explained that if they did not wish to be part of the study, the notes on their presentations and their visual data would not be used. Participation in the study meant simply giving permission to include the observation notes and the selfies from the presentation as part of the data set. It also meant agreeing to be interviewed, should it be necessary to check details that were not captured in the notes. It was explained to the students that participation was voluntary and that they could withdraw their consent at any point, without having to give a reason. They were assured that their identity would be protected and that no selfie photographs would accompany publication.

Discussion of the outcomes

As stated earlier, the original learning outcome was to encourage the students to practise their English language fluency through the selfie presentations. If their effective use of the target language to communicate is to be taken as an indication, then the intended outcome was achieved. The students had the opportunity to integrate their previously-learnt vocabulary and expressions in describing and expressing themselves. Based on observation notes taken during the presentations, the students were able to revise different forms of verb tenses – simple past, past progressive, past perfect simple, simple or progressive future, and so on – in an authentic way. The activity can also be seen to be empowering in that the students had control of which aspects of themselves they wanted to talk about. They assumed the role of knowledge experts, unlike the traditional classroom structure where the teacher is the source or transmitter of expert knowledge.

Informal coding of the visual data in the form of photographs and the accompanying oral presentations suggests that students employed the selfie for a variety of complex reasons – to share grief, make subversive statements, preserve special moments, and express the *real self* behind the selfie. Indeed, the negative portrayal of the selfie as a reflection of a narcissistic culture might have been over-simplified and reductive (Frosh, 2015; Murray, 2015). This is not to say that the students do not post selfies which are motivated by vanity or self-absorption. The point that needs to be made here is that the same person might post different selfies for a variety of complex reasons. As Murray (2015, p.499) asserts, "[t]he term selfie has complicated and reframed cultural understandings of photographic self-representation in such a way that it perverts and stigmatizes a gesture that is mobilized for a diversity of reasons."

Of the 28 students, eight took a selfie of their face only; 11 students showed family and friends in group selfies; five employed the selfie as witnessing or photojournalism (see Koliska and Roberts, 2015); and four used their photographs to make a strong statement about culture and society. A few of the illuminating selfie stories shared by the students follow:

Khim and her mother[2]
Khim showed a photograph of herself taken at a seaside restaurant with her mother, who was not in the picture, but was present in the scene. For her presentation, Khim talked about how much her mother meant to her.

Gan, missing his Dad
Gan had a photograph of himself in bed, with his eyes closed. He said that whenever he closed his eyes before he went to sleep, he felt the calming presence of his father, who died the previous year.

Nan, she ugly
Nan took a very unflattering close up selfie of herself, in black and white. She told the audience that it was her way of protesting the "like" culture of Facebook, which promotes an unrealistic goal for young women to always look pretty and slim.

Onsiri, wearing a mask

Onsiri said that what people saw outwardly was not the real her, instead just a mask. She added that she was in the process of getting to know "the real me".

Aom and her dog

Aom had a photograph of her cuddling her dog that had just died. She shed tears while telling the audience how much her dog made her happy.

The examples above indicate that the activity, initially conceptualised as a language learning exercise, did more than create a space for students to develop their oral communication fluency. Largely owing to the students' level of self-disclosure and active participation in sharing their selfie stories, social relations in the classroom were arguably enhanced, facilitating a feeling of belonging and in-group membership (Brown and Levinson, 1987). The story-telling that accompanied the face-to-face selfie presentations seemed to have contributed to strengthening personal bonds and trust between the students, as well as between the teacher and the students (Gye, 2007), giving a sense of strong community, group identity, and "phatic bonding" (Riley, 2006). For example, when Aom talked about the loss of her dog, a few of the students in the audience cried with her; some hugged her after the presentation. It would be an over-claim to state that the initiative alone suddenly changed the dynamics in the classroom. However, it is proposed that the sharing of personal narratives and feelings contributed to the strengthening of common ground and collective identity (Fant, 2001; Victoria, 2011). It is also worth pointing out that other scholars have suggested that selfies and personal photography used on an online environment do help maintain social relations (Gye, 2007; Frosh, 2015; Katz and Crocker, 2015).

Would the activity have presented a different set of results had the students simply talked about themselves without the selfie? Probably not. The selfie's ability to show the "self, enacting itself" (Frosh, 2015, p.1621) invites self-reflection perhaps because it conjures up an "extra sensation of objectivizing the self" (Carpenter, 1995, p.488). Referring to his work on photographic elicitation as a data collection method, Harper (2002, p.23) claims that using photographs in interviews seems to appeal to "deeper shafts into a different part of human consciousness than do words-alone interviews".

Furthermore, it is suggested that the very process of photographic production and selection enabled the students to "explore the taken for granted in their lives, reflecting on personal experiences through the process of image production" (Liebenberg, 2009, p.450). Instead of solely depending on language to share their stories, the selfie enriched their communicative repertoire. As Harper (2002, p.23) emphasises, photographs "capture the impossible: a person gone; an event past. That extraordinary sense of seeming to retrieve something that has disappeared belongs alone to the photograph, and it leads to deep and interesting talk."

Another selfie-inspired initiative: UK university context

Drawing from the encouraging results of the undertaking in Thailand, an altered version of the selfie activity was implemented at a UK university[3]. Unlike the Thai initiative, the UK one was not a language class and did not involve selfie oral presentations. The aim was not to provide fluency and pronunciation practise but simply to help the teacher get to know the students on an individual basis. Since the UK class was a much larger cohort – 73 second-year students, as opposed to 28 in Thailand – it was important to design an activity that would allow the teacher to build rapport with the students on an individual basis. At the beginning of the trimester, the students were asked to submit a "written selfie", in the form of self-introduction with a photograph. It was an unassessed exercise and participation was voluntary.

Mindful of the cultural diversity, the UK-based students were asked to write whatever information they felt was important for the teacher to know about them. The details of what to include in the self-introduction were intentionally left vague so that the students could decide for themselves what they considered relevant or important. The hard copy submissions were then compiled in a binder for easy access during lectures and tutorials; this binder of self-introductions with photographs functioned as an improvised version of a non-digital Facebook or photograph album with captions. It served as a handy and convenient resource of information about the individual learners – all in the flick of a page. Thus, matching students' names to their faces was effectively facilitated.

For their written selfies, the majority of the students gave information about their age, family background, hobbies, place of origin, the languages they speak, plans for the future, and their programme of study. Others included their bucket list, links to a website address of their online portfolio, films they produced, and photographs they had taken as part of other module requirements. It was quite a revelation to find out that in this cohort of students, there were three professional band members and two singers. One was a judo champion; another was a Jujitsu expert with a second degree black belt. There were other narratives: a female student whose biggest dream is to do volunteer work in Southeast Asia[4]; another wrote of her phobia of sleeping alone; one said he was not very fond of his mother's cooking. Other memorable information, which some of them referred to as "fun facts" included birthmarks of a particular shape, addiction to dark chocolate, and fear of insects. An international student disclosed her learning disability; another shared an anecdote of having grown up in a tiny village in a forest consisting of only a few households. What these self-portraits seem to suggest is that each student had a unique story to tell, and that they were eager to share it. It is proposed that they wanted to be seen as multidimensional individuals with a rich repertoire of identities, the student-identity just being one of many.

Based on experience and observation, the written selfie initiative made it much easier for the teacher to establish rapport with the students. What was really noteworthy, however, was how the activity metamorphosed into a solidarity building device, which was unplanned and unexpected: a "happy accident" (Perry and Edwards, 2010, p.1). It evolved into a useful tool for encouraging engagement and belonging, which arguably becomes more challenging in large classes (Masika and Jones, 2015). The memorable information that the students shared on their written selfies was transformed into conversation starters or ice-breakers, where a particular student could be approached and spoken to as intimates (Maynard and Zimmerman, 1984). For instance, without any preamble, a student could be asked about their opinion of a specific artist or how their part-time job at a local pub was going. Having knowledge of a piece of memorable information about a particular student made it possible to simply strike up a conversation by asking, for example, what they thought about the last episode of a BBC series. With a student who included a photograph of herself with her pet, she was often asked how the pet was doing.

It is therefore suggested that the selfie-inspired initiative has facilitated "rapid intimacy" (Victoria, 2011, p.72) between lecturer and students, and discouraged learners from hiding behind the curtain of anonymity. This resonates with Goffman's (1956) notion of the backstage where the actors can be truly themselves without worrying about the assigned roles that they were expected to play. Furthermore, since the themes of those informal conversations (usually before or right after the class, or at coffee break) were not related to the academic content of the tutorial, the student-teacher roles became less salient, thus evoking a more symmetrical power relation. It bears mentioning at this point that the self-portraits were also used to target particular students to further enhance their learning experience. As an example, students who had part-time jobs at that time would be asked how they were managing their time between university and work. The UK initiative can be likened to a "pedagogical safe house" (Canagarajah, 2004, p.121) which enabled the students to share relevant aspects of their personal background in a safe space.

Conclusion

To summarise, a language fluency exercise was designed, inspired by the Thai students' fascination with the selfie. Not only were the language learning outcomes achieved, but the selfie presentations seemed to have strengthened social bonds in the classroom, as well as encouraging self-awareness and reflexivity among the students. There was also a happy side effect in that the students enjoyed the activity and were thus fully engaged. A minor downside was that selfie presentations took longer than expected. The time allotted per student was ten minutes but the question-and-answer portion generated much discussion. The de-briefing that followed the presentations also took longer than initially planned, but was encouraged so long as the students were using the target language in their discussions. If a similar initiative were to be implemented, it is recommended that the presentations be interspersed with other planned lessons. If a formal study is the goal, it would be a good idea to have the presentations recorded. While notes were made during the presentations at the Thai university, a video or audio recording would have made for a richer set of data to be analysed. However, it should be borne in mind that any form of recording will carry its own disadvantages – students might be more inhibited, for example. Ethics approval could be sought from the start of data collection if dissemination of results is one of the end goals. On the other hand, as in the case of the Thai initiative, having the selfie activity as a regular part of the classroom task (instead of a formal research activity) would likely be less daunting for the students.

The UK initiative, which was inspired by the Thai study, was conceptualised to facilitate the management of a large class through the aid of the students' written self-portraits. A serendipitous benefit was that rapport between teacher and students was facilitated through the strategic use of personal information contained in the self-portrait. Indeed, the importance of a conducive, non-threatening learning environment along with the quality of student-teacher relationship cannot be over-emphasised as it has been found to correlate with academic achievement (Fan, 2012).

The biggest advantage of the UK initiative was that it was relatively easy to implement. It entailed asking the students to submit written self-portraits with photographs, reading them, and remembering memorable information to be used as ice-breakers or conversation starters. A possible modification to this activity might be to have the students share with each other, in groups, the contents of their self-introduction. This way, a rapport can be established not just between teacher and student but also between students. If suitable to the cultural context, a group selfie might be considered. This could include dividing the students into study groups and asking them to take a group selfie with written introductions; this might facilitate rapid intimacy, thus encouraging friendships among the students.

As a point of personal reflection from the initiatives, two things are worth emphasising. First is the importance of an ethnographic perspective: the ability to view things from the students' perspective. There were reservations in implementing the initiative in Thailand because of the negative associations surrounding the selfie. However, it was felt that to get students actively engaged, the task must incorporate elements that they found interesting, stimulating, and relatable. Second, in order to make sense of the visual data and to broaden the academic horizon, it was necessary to borrow insights from visual methodologies. Following Douglas Gauntlett (Gauntlett and Holzwarth, 2006), it is proposed that adding the visual element encouraged self-reflexivity and self-expression. The process of creating an artefact and then reflecting upon it afterward seems to "enable people to communicate in a meaningful way about their identities and experiences, and their own thoughts about their identities and experiences" (ibid, p.82).

In terms of the application of the methods used here to a wider academic practice, it is recommended that the practitioner start with an assessment of how a selfie-based activity is to be used in the classroom. As the UK and Thai initiatives show, the selfie craze is not "one single phenomenon with a singular purpose of engagement" but one that "encompasses a range of use and intention" (Katz and Crocker 2015, p.1870). Is the selfie activity to be used by the teacher to get to know the students individually, or is it for the students to get to know each other? Is it for a culturally mixed cohort? What variation of the selfie initiative would be most appropriate – written self-portrait, video selfie, or group selfie? What about an inter-class selfie to establish a friendlier community across the university? The use of different visual materials could be extended to other areas of wider practice such as in assessments (i.e. photographic essay) or recorded presentations. Further investigations are needed in order to gain more insights into how the learning and teaching environment can be enriched by combining and adapting ideas from different methodologies and media.

Mabel Victoria is a Lecturer of Intercultural Business Communication and Exploring Culture at Edinburgh Napier University. She has a PhD in Intercultural Communication and Applied Sociolinguistics, an MA in Teaching English as a Foreign Language, and an MRes in Education. She is interested in applying insights from linguistic ethnography, discourse analysis, and intercultural communication in the analysis of spoken discourse, and has published widely in this area. Her most recent publications include *Blue paint and white underwear:*

humour and misunderstanding in intercultural encounters (in press) and *English: its role as the language of comity in an employment programme for Canadian immigrants* (2014).

Notes

1. This particular class met twice a week for 1.5 hours each tutorial.

2. Pseudonyms for all students' names were used to preserve anonymity.

3. This was after the author moved to a UK university after Thailand.

4. To preserve anonymity and confidentiality, some pieces of information were made less specific, i.e. instead of mentioning the specific country, the larger geographic region was used; no specific names of places or location were mentioned.

References

Brown, P. and Levinson, S. (1987). *Politeness: Some Universals in Language Usage.* Cambridge: Cambridge University Press.

Canagarajah, S. (2004). Subversive identities, pedagogical safehouses, and critical learning. In: Norton, B. and Toohey, K. (Eds.). *Critical Pedagogies and Language Learning.* Cambridge, MA: Cambridge University Press. 116–137

Carpenter, E. (1995). The tribal terror of self awareness. In: Hockings, P. (Ed.). *Principles of Visual Ethnography.* 2nd edn. Berlin: Mouton de Gruyter. 481–491

Fan, F. A. (2012). Teacher: students' interpersonal relationships and students' academic achievements in social studies. *Teachers and Teaching: Theory and Practice*, 18 (4), 483–490 [Online]. Available at: http://doi.org/10.1080/13540 602.2012.696048 [Accessed 8 June 2016].

Fant, L. (2001). Creating awareness of identity work in conversation: a resource for language training. In: M. Kelly, L. Fant, and I. Elliot (Eds.). *Third Level, Third Space: Intercultural Communication in Language in European Higher Education.* Bern: Peter Lang. 79–93

Frosh, P. (2015). The gestural image: the selfie, photography theory, and Kinesthetic sociability. *International Journal of Communication*, 9, 1607–1628.

Gauntlett, D., and Holzwarth, P. (2006). Creative and visual methods for exploring identities. *Visual Studies*, 21 (1), 82–91 [Online]. Available at: http://doi.org/10.1080/14725860600613261 [Accessed 9 February 2016].

Giroux, H. A. (2015). Selfie culture in the age of corporate and state surveillance. *Third Text*, 29 (3), 155–164 [Online]. Available at: http://doi.org/10.1080/095 28822.2015.1082339 [Accessed 9 February 2016].

Goffman, E. (1956). *The Presentation of Self in Everyday Life.* Edinburgh: University of Edinburgh [Online]. Available at: http://doi.org/10.2307/258197 [Accessed 5 February 2016].

Gye, L. (2007). Picture this: the impact of mobile camera phones on personal photographic practices. *Continuum*, 21 (2), 279–288 [Online]. Available at: http://doi.org/10.1080/10304310701269107 [Accessed 6 February 2016].

Hammersley, M. and Atkinson, P. (2007). *Ethnography: Principles in Practice.* 3rd edn. London: Routledge.

Harper, D. (2002). Talking about pictures: a case for photo elicitation. *Visual Studies*, 17 (1), 13–26 [Online]. Available at: http://doi. org/10.1080/14725860220137345 [Accessed 17 October 2015].

Iqani, M. and Schroeder, J. E. (2015). #selfie: digital self-portraits as commodity form and consumption practice. *Consumption Markets and Culture* [Online]. Available at: http://doi.org/10.1080/10253866.2015.1116784 [Accessed 9 February 2016].

Katz, J. E. and Crocker, E. T. (2015). Selfies and photo messaging as visual conversation: reports from the United States, United Kingdom and China. *International Journal of Communication*, 9, 1861–1872.

Koliska, M. and Roberts, J. (2015). Selfies: witnessing and participatory journalism with a point of view. [Online]. Available at: http://ijoc.org/index. php/ijoc/article/viewFile/3149/1392 [Accessed 29 May 2015].

Liebenberg, L. (2009). The visual image as discussion point: increasing validity in boundary crossing research. *Qualitative Research*, 9 (4), 441–467. [Online]. Available at: http://doi.org/10.1177/1468794109337877 [Accessed 19 February 2016].

Masika, R. and Jones, J. (2015). Building student belonging and engagement: insights into higher education students' experiences of participating and learning together. *Teaching in Higher Education*, 21 (2), 138–150. [Online]. Available at: http://doi.org/10.1080/13562517.2015.1122585 [Accessed 12 February 2016].

Maynard, D. W. and Zimmerman, D. H. (1984). Topical talk, ritual and the social organization of relationships. *Social Psychology Quarterly*, 47 (4), 301–316 [Online]. Available at: http://doi.org/10.2307/3033633 [Accessed 17 September 2015].

Murray, D. C. (2015). Notes to self: the visual culture of selfies in the age of social media. *Consumption Markets & Culture*, 18 (6), 490–516. [Online]. Available at: http://doi.org/10.1080/10253866.2015.1052967 [Accessed 6 February 2016].

Nation, P. (1989). Improving speaking fluency. *System*, 17 (3), 377–384.

Perry, B., and Edwards, M. (2010). Encyclopedia of case study research. In Mills, A. J., Durepos, G., and Wiebe, E. (Eds.). *Encyclopedia of Case Study Research.* Thousand Oaks: Sage Publications [Online]. Available at: http://doi.org/10.4135/9781412957397 [Accessed 18 February 2016].

Riley, P. (2006). Self-expression and the negotiation of identity in a foreign language. *International Journal of Applied Linguistics*, 16 (3), 295–318. [Online]. Available at: http://doi.org/10.1111/j.1473-4192.2006.00120.x [Accessed 13 June 2015].

Senft, T. M. and Baym, N. K. (2015). What does the selfie say? Investigating a global phenomenon introduction. *International Journal of Communication*, 9, 1588–1606. [Online]. Available at: ijoc.org [Accessed 15 February 2016].

Victoria, M. (2011). Building common ground in intercultural encounters: a study of classroom interaction in an employment preparation programme for Canadian immigrants. PhD thesis: The Open University.

Victoria, M. P. (2011). Ethical dimensions of shared ethnicity, language, and immigration experience. *TESL Canada Journal*, 28 (5), 72–79.

Wortham, J. (2013). My selfie, myself. *The New York Times*, 1–5. [Online]. Available at: http://www.nytimes.com/2013/10/20/sunday-review/my-selfie-myself.html [Accessed 2 February 2016].

Zinn, C. and Scheuer, O. (2006). Getting to know your students in distance learning contexts. In Nejdl, W. and Tochtermann, K. (Eds.). *Innovative Approaches for Learning and Knowledge Sharing.* Berlin: Springer. 437–451. [Online]. Available at: http://doi.org/10.1007/11876663_34 [Accessed 21 February 2016].

4

Developing a global outlook through pedagogical activities

Empowering peer-to-peer learning communities in a global online classroom

Rachel Younger

ABSTRACT

In answer to the observation by Laurillard (2012) that Western universities have not integrated a multicultural dimension in their curricula, this chapter contends that peer-to-peer exchange among distance learners from diverse cultural backgrounds is a key tool in promoting a culturally diverse approach to online education. The value of interaction and collaboration amongst peers in the specific context of a distance Master's (MA) degree in International Journalism is the focus of a case study in this chapter.

This MA brings together professionally active students from across the globe. The curriculum is designed to facilitate knowledge sharing in lieu of knowledge *export*. Students from a range of cultural contexts compare perspectives and experiences, and collaborate on group projects. The curriculum enables them not only to reflect upon, but also to experience culturally diverse approaches to their profession. Correspondingly, this case study demonstrates how an internationalisation of the curriculum could be achieved if collaborative peer-to-peer communities were empowered.

Keywords: journalism education, internationalisation, distance learning, peer-to-peer communities

Introduction

This chapter will reflect on the value of peer-to-peer learning, applied in the context of a distance Master's in International Journalism. In its three years of existence, the global online classroom of this MA has united media professionals and journalists based in over 30 nations and in six world regions. These journalists and media professionals work for known global media outlets such as Al Jazeera, Reuters, BBC, CNN, Sky, ITN, France 24, Arte, IPC Media, Forbes, Spiegel, and local media around the globe; they also have roles as communications and information officers within global organisations such as the UN, the World Bank, the European Union, and the International Court of Justice.

Studies on this degree are flexible, with students able to tailor assignments to support their individual career objectives. They can study at a pace of their choosing, and during hours of the week that suit them. The flexible curriculum is designed to support the career progression of busy professionals. Interaction among peers in the global online classroom aims to encourage innovation of professional practice, and also to enhance the global mobility of each participant. It is this final outcome that is the focus of this paper: the ability of students to adapt journalistic content for diverse global audiences, and to exercise their professional practice comfortably within a range of international contexts.

In the following, a call by journalism educators for a more international outlook within journalism studies will be discussed, as well as a call by distance learning experts for an increased focus on the community aspect of online learning. This paper will argue that an increased focus on peer-to-peer learning can indeed promote a called-for internationalisation of the curriculum. It will further outline how the aforementioned distance MA makes use of the community aspect of online learning to achieve precisely this aim.

The case for de-Westernising and internationalising journalism studies

Academics widely recognise that the professional values of journalists around the globe differ, and that there are also global differences in the practice of journalism. *The Global Journalist in the 21ˢᵗ Century*, for example, features surveys conducted amongst 29,000 journalists in 31 countries by 80 authors. The editors of this mammoth compilation of single-nation surveys conclude with this argument:

> What seems certain is that a culture of global journalism has not yet emerged. Just as the first edition of the *Global Journalist* concluded more than 13 years ago, the second edition found little evidence of a trend towards a global journalism culture. [...] Most of the research reviewed in this book shows that journalistic values and norms depend heavily on social, political, and cultural contexts (Weaver and Willnat 2012, p.546).

Hanitzsch (2012), the chair of a series of comparative studies united under the heading *Worlds of Journalism Study* – conducted by academics based in over 70 countries – identifies some common professional values many journalists around the globe agree on, for example: detachment, non-involvement, reliability, and use of factual information. On the other hand, journalists around the globe differ in their views on interventionist aspects of journalism such as advocacy journalism, and in their views on the role of subjectivity versus objectivity in reporting (ibid, p.492).

Whilst a genuinely collaborative approach to global journalism research is spreading, it was not originally taken for granted. Halloran (1998) and Josephi (2005) cited in Hanitzsch (2007) have criticised the manner in which research methodologies that were originally designed to better understand Western journalism were then applied to African, Asian, or Latin American contexts in an act of Western research imperialism.

Amongst those calling for a stronger focus on global differences in the academic field of journalism are: Deuze (2001), who argues for a stronger awareness of multiculturalism in journalism; Josephi (2005), who challenges the dominant Anglo-American academic view of journalism; Wasserman and de Beer (2009), who call for a de-Westernisation of both journalism research and journalism studies; and finally Papoutsaki (2007), who calls for a "de-colonisation" of journalism curricula. Likewise, The World Journalism Education Congress scheduled for July 2016 issued a call for papers on "Global perspectives: De-Westernising journalism education".

This paper aims to discuss the value of global online learning communities, and the role peer-to-peer interaction within these communities can play in achieving de-Westernisation and internationalisation of journalism studies. The distance MA that will serve as case study was designed with a genuinely global perspective on journalism in mind. Peer-to-peer learning in the global online classroom is a key tool employed to facilitate the delivery of a multicultural, de-Westernised curriculum.

As Hanitzsch contends, "… cultures are often evaluated through the lens of the researchers' cultural value systems. The only way to overcome ethnocentrism is through collaborative research" (2007, p.96). Along the same lines, this paper will argue that only through collaborative learning among peers from around the globe will ethnocentrism in learning be overcome.

Whilst the focus of this paper is the internationalisation of journalism education, comparable principles apply to other fields of study. As Laurillard points out, in the context of rising overseas student numbers on Western distance degrees, "the Western university system has stuck resolutely to Western-oriented curricula, and has not really taken advantage of the multicultural opportunities these changes could have provided" (2012, p.41). This paper will demonstrate how such multicultural opportunities can be exploited in the context of distance learning.

The value of peer-to-peer learning in online communities

Education theorists make strong arguments for strengthening the community aspect of distance learning. Garrison and Anderson (2003) point out that "community is integral to all aspects of life", and that "this is no less so from an educational perspective". Rather than learning being an individual experience, "education and learning in its best sense is a collaboration, which includes a sense of belonging and acceptance in a group with common interests" (ibid, p.49). Likewise, Palloff and Pratt (2013) agree that interaction amongst students is key to the learning process, and paying attention to community is "not just fluff, or something extra that already overburdened instructors need to pay attention to". As they point out, focusing on the community aspect of learning can "infuse teaching with new energy and passion" (ibid, p.28).

Laurillard (2012) describes learning activities that do not necessarily require interaction amongst peers, such as acquisition of knowledge, inquiry, practice, or production. She compares these with inherently interactive forms of learning, such as discussion and collaboration, and highlights the social value of the peer group as a means for motivating and enabling the learning process:

> The group is valuable to each of its members because it makes demands on them to produce a contribution to the group goal. In the process of doing so, the learner has to construct an idea, explanation or description. This idea is then available to the others to challenge or modify, and for the originator to defend or redevelop (ibid, p.189).

If students are required to interact with peers to negotiate a shared understanding of the world, this will motivate them to engage in deeper forms of learning as they construct, articulate, defend, and challenge their mental models of the world. As a consequence, Laurillard argues that "collaborative learning is a powerful form of learning" (ibid, p.57).

Palloff and Pratt (2013) agree that when students engage in peer-to-peer learning, they "collaborate to create new knowledge and meaning", resulting in "deeper levels of reflection and a stronger sense of having learned" (ibid, p.28). They argue that:

> Collaborative learning processes help students achieve deeper levels of knowledge generation through the creation of shared goals, shared exploration, and a shared process of meaning making. In addition, collaborative activity can help reduce the feelings of isolation that can occur when students are working at a distance (ibid, p.39).

Garrison and Anderson (2003) equally highlight the value of a critical community of inquiry in promoting the construction of "deep and meaningful learning" as well as genuine critical discourse; they point out that "a community of learners is an essential, core element of an educational experience when higher-order learning is the desired outcome" (ibid, p.22).

Whilst Laurillard (2012) observes that active and collaborative learning techniques – where students work on projects together – have "been found to result in stronger student engagement" (ibid, p.47), Palloff and Pratt (2013) have also found that "when collaboration is not encouraged, participation in the online course is generally low" (ibid, p.39).

If collaborative learning is the goal, then it is "e-learning's unique ability to bring together a community of learners, unrestricted by time or place that must be understood" (Garrison and Anderson 2003, p.12). The authors argue that communication technologies such as computer conferencing "can enhance the quality of learning outcomes in higher education by increasing access to critical communities of learners, not simply access to information" (ibid, p.24). Selwyn (2011) also agrees that one of the defining characteristics of modern online technologies lies in their focus on "collective actions of communities of users, rather than individuals" (ibid, p.14). Many digital technologies "allow learning to take place within collaborative and supportive social contexts and fit neatly with the [...] view that learning often best takes place as a social process of collective knowledge construction" (ibid, p.26). Selwyn, who describes learning as a "profoundly social process" (ibid, p.76), points out that "the notion of learning as a collaborative and socially situated process has found particular resonance with many academics working in the area of educational technology," as "digital technologies can act as powerful social resources in an individual's learning context" (ibid, p.77).

However, Garrison and Anderson (2003) would disagree. In their view, "the educational community has barely begun to appreciate the collaborative capabilities of e-learning and, as a result, these capabilities are greatly underutilised" (ibid, p.22). They also argue "implicit denial of community has perhaps been the greatest shortcoming of traditional distance education with its focus on prescriptive course packages, to be assimilated by the student in isolation" (ibid, p.49).

The distance MA in International Journalism – the focus of this case study – has been noted for its strong emphasis on community, and on peer-to-peer and collaborative learning. It is the contention of this paper that interaction among peers from across the globe (with its resultant access to a rich multitude of global perspectives on journalism) is one of the greatest assets of this distance MA. A strong focus on this community of peers plays a key role in ensuring that the curriculum is genuinely international.

How to empower peer-to-peer learning communities in practice?

As has been outlined above, one main goal of the curriculum design for this Master's degree was to facilitate and encourage peer-to-peer interaction within the community of learners, specifically with the aim to strengthen the ability of students to operate globally. Opportunities to exchange cross-cultural perspectives on theory and practice are woven into the fabric of the curriculum on several levels, as will now be discussed.

Sharing global perspectives on academic theory

In weekly chat forums on the course intranet, students debate academic research into differences in journalistic practice around the globe. The emphasis is on each student sharing their individual experience of applications to each theory in their own country. In one exercise, for example, students compare different codes of journalism ethics in a range of countries around the globe. They then share the ethical values to which the journalistic community in their own country adheres. Finally, they take the exercise one step further and discuss with their peers which ethical guidelines they would include in a new code of journalism ethics for a fictional country named *Newland*.

These online debates tend to be more engaging if a different student is assigned every week to begin the debate with a short video presentation, and to facilitate that week's debate as forum host. Once students have dismissed the idea that academics are the only ones to contribute knowledge and expertise to the learning process, the doors are open to everyone benefiting from the diverse wisdom of the crowd in the global online classroom.

During such online debates, students have shared their views and experiences with notions like objectivity, impartiality, or news values. Students also differ on whether journalists should see themselves as neutral watchdogs of political and financial elites, or instead exercise interventionist forms of journalism such as advocacy journalism or peace journalism. Sometimes these views are influenced by the geopolitical contexts in which students operate. Restrictive media laws that require them to tread wisely for the sake of their own personal safety also play a role.

Peer-to-peer feedback on students' individual professional practice

On several modules within the programme, students produce substantial individual journalistic artefacts: for example, a cross-platform blog, a documentary film, or a major journalistic investigation. The production process is broken down into weekly milestones and students are expected to post regular updates on (or links to) their draft work in weekly forums in the global online classroom.

Students are naturally inclined to seek individual feedback on draft work from the module tutor who has a relevant specialist professional background. Whenever students email lecturers for individual guidance, tutors systematically refer them back to the weekly forum; here they get advice and feedback from the tutor but, more essentially, also from peers based around the globe.

As a consequence, students as well as academic staff are exposed to a globally diverse range of approaches to production. In one online forum – in which students commented on their peers' draft documentary films – an interesting debate about the definition of the word *documentary* was inspired by a particularly poetic film produced in Sudan. The producer of the documentary was living in a high context culture (Hall, 1976), where people tend to express things between the lines rather than explicitly; this made her poetic narrative style a natural choice. Fellow students from low context cultures, where communication is more explicit, were intrigued by this alternative approach to storytelling.

Peer-to-peer feedback on individual coursework in progress does more than promote a better understanding of global differences in production. An important benefit of the community aspect of learning is also the mutual encouragement and joint brainstorming of solutions that takes place in weekly online forums. In the context of students producing individual cross-platform blogs that showcase their specialist areas of expertise, mutual compliments and suggestions go a long way to uphold morale. Regular group interaction also engenders an element of friendly competitiveness, which results in better final journalistic artefacts. There have been several instances of students' innovative industry practice having been inspired by discussions in the global online classroom.

A major question for anyone delivering a cross-platform journalism MA online is how to teach technical skills. On campus, technical tutors or academics would be able to demonstrate to students how to operate a camera, how to work with video editing software, or how to stream a social media feed onto a blog. Distance students on this MA are not only commenting on their peers' journalism, but also exchanging technical how-to tips, and working together to resolve individual technical challenges: from choice of kit or operation of software to the practicalities of cross-platform production in world regions with regular power cuts or patchy broadband widths. Here again, group morale motivates particularly technophobic students to problem-solve and innovate; a valuable skill in an industry with ever-evolving technological realities.

Adapting journalistic content for a diverse range of overseas audiences

For some years now, the global journalism industry has seen a decline in full-time, long-term employment. Professionals are increasingly expected to become entrepreneurs who freelance across several platforms. They are under pressure to expand their markets internationally and to adapt content for both local and overseas markets. To help students further develop their global mobility – their ability to operate internationally – they are required to produce content for one national market of choice, to refashion it for an audience in a different world region, and then to reflect on how they adapted the story and why.

As Weaver and Willnat (2012) point out, whilst a great deal of research has been carried out into role perceptions, norms, and values of journalists around the globe, less academic attention has been paid to how these beliefs influence their actual work. Whilst tutors can introduce students to some global differences in reporting, not all of them have yet been explored by the academic community. Why not get students involved in the ongoing, collaborative, global effort to better understand how journalistic content might ideally be adapted for specific overseas audiences?

When students are thrown in at the deep end and asked to adapt content for two very diverse regions, the usual response is a request for guidance from academic staff. Tutors refer students back to the peer-to-peer learning community; the discoveries they make as a result tend to be very interesting. For example, a student from Nigeria showed his copy to a fellow learner based in the UK. The latter felt he needed to include far more wit and entertainment in his piece to engage a UK audience. Another student showed a TV report he had produced for a UK broadcaster to a peer from the United States. The feedback he got was to edit the piece down to a shorter and faster-paced version to suit an American audience. A third student wrote a piece of watchdog journalism for a European and a Middle Eastern audience, and obtained feedback from colleagues in the Middle East on repackaging part of the information in a less explicit form that would not create legal issues.

Several academic studies, including *The Worlds of Journalism* studies spearheaded by Hanitzsch (2007), have demonstrated different approaches to market-orientation and the use of entertainment in journalism, or differences in journalistic power distance – the willingness of journalists to be adversarial in specific journalistic cultures. There is nothing like personal experimentation with these theories in a peer-to-peer context to help students make their content travel around the globe more effectively.

Co-production in a global virtual newsroom

Many on-campus journalism degrees across the UK operate regular live roll-ing news days, during which students report news of the day from Parliament, the courts, local businesses, and a wide spectrum of the local community. Interaction between students on a group project of this nature provides a val-uable opportunity to practice essential skills, including teamwork, production to high standards under pressure, news judgment, and conflict management.

With comparable learning outcomes in mind, students on this distance MA assemble in a global virtual newsroom to design and produce a joint cross-platform website from scratch. The one difference is that their contri-butions are made from around the globe, where they are based, and aim to be relevant to diverse and global audiences. The negotiation of topics and news values, the scheduling of output, subediting, quality control and the multitude of other activities relevant to a global news operation take place online, with nobody physically present in the same place at the same time.

It is during group work in such a global virtual newsroom where stu-dents' wide range of journalistic values and approaches to practice are tried and tested most: under pressure, in direct interaction with their peers. Students experience first-hand the difference between what Trompenaars and Hampden Turner (1997) would call a "sequential" or "synchronic" approach to time management, with some students adhering to deadlines more dili-gently than others. They experience what Hofstede (1980) would call "high power distance" versus "low power distance" approaches to management and leadership, where some peers adopt a more – and others a less – democratic approach to decision making. Some will interpret the low-context, explicit feedback of their peers, voiced under pressure, as blunt or even insulting; others will not pick up on the subtler, between-the-lines comments voiced by their more implicit, high-context peers.

To make use again of dimensions defined by Hanitzsch (2007), these group co-productions, with contributors based around the globe, also provide an ideal opportunity to discuss whether the joint product will treat the intended global target audience more as citizens or consumers; whether analysis and reason or evidence and fact will play a larger role; whether the reporting style will be more or less interventionist; whether the tone of reporting will be more or less confrontational or, to use Hanitzsch's description, adversarial. It is relatively easy to chat about diverse approaches to journalism in the safe environment of a chat forum, but there is more at stake for individuals when the group is working to a tight deadline, and the resulting product is assessed with one single group mark for all. This pressure often brings out the more individualist or collectivist worldview that different members of the group identify with (Hofstede, 1980).

Travelling for overseas content and the alumni network

Although it is not compulsory, many students opt to travel overseas for the production of one or a few of their assessed journalistic artefacts. Some students also opt to complete work placements with overseas media companies. Everything they learn from lectures, online debates, peer feedback on their work, or interaction during group projects is tested and tried at a deeper level, as students immerse themselves in an environment they are less familiar with.

Students at all levels of journalistic production are trained in and expected to engage with rigorous risk assessment. It is all the more important for students who travel overseas. Distance students have access to the same wide range of training materials provided to on-campus students on assessing and mitigating risk, for both home and overseas production. In addition to this, however, they often have the benefit of one of their peers having lived or worked in the world region they are planning to travel to. Students often help each other with local information, which can include knowledge of local customs and sensitivities, and with useful contacts.

Studies on this distance MA are flexible, and students can take between one year (full time) and two to four years (part time) to complete their degree. Some students take up studies in January, others in May. As a consequence, a central online hub for students to spend time socially and to mingle with peers who do not happen to be on the same module at the same time has turned out to be important. The most intuitive environment for this is Facebook, as this enables alumni to remain part of the wider global community of professionals after they have graduated. This is the location where many students collect additional advice on their destination of overseas production, sometimes from peers they have not yet formally studied with. This is also an informal space where students often choose to celebrate their overseas experiences by posting photos and live-rolling trip updates of a more social nature.

It was during one of these overseas trips that a student encouraged the teaching team to take the peer-to-peer community concept one step further. Whilst in the context of his studies – he was on work experience with a global news organisation based in London – the devastating attack on the Bataclan Theatre in Paris occurred. The student had started documenting his work experience in London in a video diary; he continued to produce it whilst in Paris for a few days to cover this event live for his home employer. This behind-the-scenes video was so illuminating that the course team is now encouraging all students to produce video diaries of their experiences with overseas production, completed as part of their coursework. Looking to the long-term future, these will add up to form a geographically and culturally diverse resource bank of experiences with global reporting, available to future generations of students (shared with permission of the students in question).

Needless to say, the course Facebook group is a valuable resource in itself. Not only do peers connect socially and professionally across different years of entry, but more importantly, our alumni stay in touch with each other, with academic staff, and with future students long after graduation. Both students and alumni continue to help each other by posting tips and industry-relevant news to the group page. This is peer-to-peer engagement as a long-term habit. Some one-off guest speakers, themselves high profile journalists based around the globe, have also asked to join this alumni community on Facebook. This too expands peer-to-peer learning beyond the online classroom and beyond the artificial time limit of graduation.

Lessons learnt about facilitating peer-to-peer learning communities

The general consensus amongst faculty and students is that peer-to-peer learning in the global online classroom is worth encouraging. Students will need to be reminded time and again to share with their peers, and to see them as a learning resource that is as important as academic staff, their lectures, or the library. The more that students and academics alike engage with this global community aspect of learning, the more skilled they become at surfing the waves of global diversity. De-Westernisation and internationalisation of journalism studies is a genuine outcome.

One lesson learnt is that online learning technologies do not need to be complicated to be effective. Tutors do post video lectures alongside book chapters and journal articles to the online learning environment, and students are required to produce journalistic content across all multimedia platforms imaginable, including social media. However, one of the key secrets to success is the technological simplicity of the global online classroom. In any given week, when students log on, they will find a video lecture, some chapters to read, some links to outside materials, and usually two chat forums – on that week's debate (in order to debate theory) and that week's task (in order to enable peer-to-peer feedback on individual productions).

Whilst students do host individual journalistic artefacts on a range of social platforms available to the general public (their blogs on WordPress, or their documentaries on Vimeo, for example), they always link their work back to the one-stop-shop weekly forum so they can share it with their peers for feedback. The majority of students on this programme are busy professionals; the less effort required to find their peers, the more likely it is they will engage in regular conversation with them in the global online learning community.

People often ask why the more sophisticated learning technologies are not used on this programme. Multiple software were tested enabling students to engage in live online conversation whilst simultaneously watching a live online lecture with slides and an interactive white board. As it turns out, however, students naturally gravitate towards more simple learning environments that mirror what they are used to on social media.

The chat forums used are similar to Facebook, with the option to post multimedia objects and comments, but also with the option to log on whenever one wishes. The students have indicated that the possibility to engage in asynchronous discussions (whenever suits the student) is important. This means a student in Australia might be chatting with a student in the Middle East overnight, and by the time a lecturer in the UK wakes up and logs on again, a whole world of activities has taken place.

Needless to say, students will only feel comfortable to share their opinions, interact with their peers, and accept frank feedback if certain ground rules help facilitate a safe and welcoming environment. All students are expected to respect diversity, race, gender, religion, disability, and age. Students are also expected to treat information shared as confidential, especially as students on this MA are global journalists working for competing organisations. This requirement for confidentiality is all the more pertinent as several of these students live and work in geopolitical contexts where indiscretion could impact their safety. There are some circumstances where students need to protect their work from the public sphere with a password or an alias. Mutual trust is a key ingredient of any functional online learning community.

Another ground rule for any thriving global online learning community must be mentioned – it should be fun! Students must be allowed to complain to their peers about the day they have been having. Peers need to be able to laugh and cry together about their frustrations with unfamiliar technologies. They should celebrate successes with each other. The experience of the teaching team has been that students are in fact naturally helpful, constructive, trustworthy, and fabulously intelligent and entertaining as they engage in sharing professional experiences and views with each other.

Successful online peer-to-peer learning is not simply about clever curriculum design or technology; it is about attitudes. Do academics and students alike genuinely welcome the rich diversity of practice that exists around the globe? Are participants interested in not only sharing valuable lessons they have learnt wherever they are based, but also in taking inspiration from those cultures they are less familiar with? Academic staff teaching on this distance degree feel privileged to have regular access to such a wealth of information about diverse forms of professional practice around the globe.

Possible future developments

As was mentioned already, the global participants in the community of learners on this distance MA are practitioners with a minimum of one year, and (at time of writing) up to 30 years of professional experience. Several students on this degree are editors or senior reporters working for major global media organisations. As Weaver and Willnat (2012, p.545) point out:

> So far, media scholars have done an impressive job of analysing how journalists consider their profession and their daily work. [...] What they have not done, however, is investigate whether and how these beliefs influence the work of journalists around the world.

This call for a renewed focus on diverse journalism practices, rather than just diverse journalistic role-perceptions, is addressed to the academic community. What if professionals as well as academics were to participate in this ambitious feat, to systematically analyse global variations of journalistic practice?

Hanitzsch (2012, p.492) joins Weaver and Willnat's call for collaborative research into professional practice:

> [...] large-scale collaborative research is a feasible and effective avenue in the field of journalism research. In fact, working on [*Worlds of Journalism*] convinced us that collaboration is a key to future attempts of contextualising our knowledge about the diversity of journalism cultures.

A desirable future development is to engage communities of professional online learners in collaborative, systematic, academic research of this nature. Peer-to-peer interaction between academia and the global professional community can only further advance the goal of many to de-Westernise and internationalise journalism studies.

Rachel Younger is a foreign correspondent and filmmaker who has reported from locations as diverse as the former Soviet Union, Brazil's favelas, Malaysia's paradise islands, the Swiss parliament and the Middle East in crisis. Since joining academia in 2004, Rachel has led programmes and been involved in curriculum design. She is Programme Leader of MA International Journalism for Media Professionals and lectures on Global Current Affairs, Documentary Film Production, Cross-platform Journalism and TV Journalism at Edinburgh Napier University. Her main research interests are cross-cultural issues in journalism and audio-visual narratives across cultures.

References

Deuze, M. (2001). Journalism education and multiculturalism: mnhancing the curriculum. *Asia Pacific Media Educator*, 10, 127–147.

Garrison, D. and Anderson, T. (2003). *E-Learning in the 21ˢᵗ Century: A Framework for Research and Practice*. London: Routledge.

Hall, E. (1976). *Beyond Culture*. New York: Anchor Books.

Halloran, J. (1998). Social science, communication research and the Third World. *Media Development*, 2, 43–46.

Hanitzsch, T. (2007). Deconstructing journalism culture: towards a universal theory. *Communication Theory*, 17 (4), 367–385.

Hanitzsch, T. et al. (Ed.) (2012). Worlds of journalism: journalistic cultures, professional autonomy and perceived influences across 18 nations. In: Weaver, D. and Willnat, L. (Eds.). *The Global Journalist in the 21ˢᵗ Century*. London: Routledge, 473–494.

Hofstede, G. (1980). *Culture's Consequences: International Differences in Work*. Beverly Hills: Sage Publications.

Hofstede, G. (1992). *Cultures and Organisations: Software of the mind*. London: Harper Collins.

Josephi, B. (2005). Journalism in the global age: between normative and empirical. *International Communications Gazette*, 67 (6), 575–590.

Laurillard, D. (2012). *Teaching as a Design Science: Building Pedagogical Patterns for Learning and Technology*. London: Routledge.

Palloff, R. and Pratt, K. (2013). *Lessons from the Virtual Classroom: The Realities of Online Teaching*. San Francisco: Jossey-Bass.

Papoutsaki, E. (2007). De-colonising journalism curricula: a research and "development" perspective. Paper presented at the Annual Conference of the Asian Media Information and Communication Centre, Singapore. [Online]. Available at http://unitec.researchbank.ac.nz/handle/10652/1503 [Accessed 20 April 2016]

Selwyn, N. (2011). *Education and Technology: Key issues and debates*. London: Continuum.

Trompenaars, F. and Hampden-Turner, C. (1997). *Riding the Waves of Culture*. London: Nicholas Brealey Publishing.

Wasserman, H. and de Beer, A. (2009). Towards de-Westernising journalism studies. In: Hanitzsch, T. and Wahl-Jorgensen, K. (Eds.). *The Handbook of Journalism Studies*. London: Routledge, 428–438.

Webb, G. (2005). Internationalisation of Curriculum an Institutional Approach. In: Carroll, J. and Ryan, J. (Eds.). *Teaching International Students: Improving Learning for All.* Routledge: Abingdon, 109–118.

Weaver, D. (Ed.). (1998). *The Global Journalist: News People Around the World.* Cresskill, NJ: Hampton.

Weaver, D. and Willnat, L. (Eds.). (2012). *The Global Journalist in the 21ˢᵗCentury.* London: Routledge.

Developing new perspectives on graphic design pedagogy and global citizenship through international volunteering

Myrna MacLeod and Iain Macdonald

ABSTRACT

Within the field of graphic design, many contemporary designers and educators seek to challenge global corporate homogenisation and the exploitation of developing countries. In an increasingly global economy students must develop an awareness of themselves and other cultures. Within the field of design education, researchers argue that design is a transformative and socially engaged practice offering an important platform for student internationalisation.

This chapter analyses how five UK design students negotiated and participated in the implementation of live projects in Mozambique. The study also examines the effect of the project on students who remained at home, but followed the work by engaging with a live blog online. The aim was to explore whether a shared cultural learning experience – through volunteering in a very different environment, with challenging resources and social conditions – would develop student global citizenship and mobility, and offer alternative approaches to graphic design career development and professional practice.

The study found that the experience did change student perspectives on how they could form a meaningful career in design by using their skills in a socially responsible way abroad. It also highlights another form of internationalisation that, through volunteering, can be embedded into design programmes and result in building relationships with third sector organisations in the developing world.

Keywords: volunteering, citizenship, international, graphic design

Introduction

Sanga Moses grew up in one of the poorest villages in Uganda. He did not wear shoes until he was 13. He went on to study business administration at university, and was the first member of his family to do so. When he graduated, he set up Eco-Fuel Africa with just $200. The social enterprise produces clean, cheap cooking fuel and organic fertiliser for poverty-stricken rural regions like the one where he was born.

Sanga designed an innovative process in which agricultural waste is converted into organic charcoal briquettes, providing a regular supply of fertiliser to farmers and clean, cheap, and safe cooking fuel to local communities. He created jobs within an innovative, sustainable business meeting energy needs, and addressed an important health issue – the fact that "[every] year more than one and a half million Africans die from indoor air pollution, often having been poisoned from the noxious fumes of makeshift cooking fuel" (Rawsthorn, 2013, p.219).

In 2011, he reached out for help to find a way of packaging the briquettes, so they could more easily be carried for long distances. Supply chain and resources were limited in Uganda, so the solution had to be produced easily and cheaply in that part of the world.

Two graphic design students solved the problem, designing a sturdy, paper drawstring sack to hold the light briquettes, which has now been in production since 2012 (see figure 1). The students did not meet Sanga Moses, but were briefed on the project by a Scottish Non-Governmental Organisation (NGO), and sent their ideas to Moses for consideration by email. When the design work was completed, by way of thanks he sent a poem.

> You have touched our lives with your kindness;
> We want to tell you "Thank you" but it doesn't seem enough.
> Words don't seem sufficient – "Blah, blah" and all that stuff.
> Please know we have deep feelings about your generous act.
> We really appreciate you – you guys are special, and that's a fact!
> Thank you, thank you so much.
>
> (Sanga Moses)

Alice Rawsthorn, influential design critic of *The International Herald Tribune* and the *New York Times* showcased the above work in *Hello World – Where Design Meets Life* (Rawsthorn, 2013). In the university's studios, the horizons of graphic design students were considerably expanded, and a new philosophy was embedded in the programme – one of using design skills in a socially responsible way, in an intercultural context. Students were able to see how "[education] plays a vital role in preparing design students to move beyond a purely reactive state to one in which they are actively engaged in shaping the world around them" (Mendoza and Matyók, 2013, p.215).

The above project also highlighted current thinking in both design education and professional practice. As Berman suggests (2009, p.39), "Rather than sharing our cycles of style, consumption, and chemical addictions, designers can use their professional power, persuasive skills, and wisdom to help distribute ideas that the world really needs: health information, conflict resolution, tolerance, technology, freedom of the press, freedom of speech, human rights, democracy…"

Figure 1: Paper sack produced by design students for a project in Uganda.

Context – The role of design in society

As economies become globally connected, there is growing pressure for higher education to develop student intercultural awareness and global citizenship (Brooks and Waters, 2011; Waters, Brooks and Pimlott-Wilson, 2011). The critical contexts influencing the creative work discussed in this chapter are set out in McCoy (1994), Poynor (1999), Mau (2004), Berman (2009) and Rawsthorn (2013).

The issue of how graphic designers use their skills in professional practice has been debated, and has influenced design pedagogy for some time. "Designers have enormous power to influence how we see our world – change our world and live our lives" (Berman 2009, p.7). This statement is true to an extent, but designers cannot do it alone, or without an understanding of the world they are attempting to change. Students are taught that design has an important role to play in our contemporary world – that they are members of a subjective practice, located in a larger social field of collaboration, influence, responsibility, participation, creativity, and reflection.

Using live graphic design projects – specifically, the creation of branding materials for small business – this chapter explores the impact of the work of five student volunteers and two tutors who travelled to Mozambique to implement their design work with the help of an NGO and several local students. Participants from both countries developed a range of intercultural competencies and new perspectives. The project provided a new platform for staff and student mobility, and for the internationalisation of coursework.

During the four weeks in rural Mozambique, the students worked along-side local students, developing shared working practices to create branding materials and publicity for the SHINE soap cooperative and the LIFE Film Festival. The *First Things First Manifesto* (Garland, 1964) provides an approach that can culturally inform the students in this study as they actively shape the world around them. Here, a vital distinction was made between the singular, commercial role of graphic design and "the possibility […] that design might have broader purposes, potential and meanings" (ibid, p.5).

Teaching strategies in design disciplines have developed around – and are simultaneously directed towards – culturally and socially appropriate, collaborative design pedagogies and artefacts. Design educators play the role of social agents. They integrate the complexities of society into spaces of reflective learning and nurture diverse pedagogical approaches, stimulating the next generation of designers to become agents of change.

In the autumn of 1999, the newly re-drafted *First Things First Manifesto* appeared in at least six journals, including *Emigre*, *AIGA Journal of Graphic Design 5*, and *Adbusters* in North America; *Eye* and *Blueprint* in the UK; and *Items* (and, much later, *Form*) on the European continent. It carried Ken Garland's name once more, augmented by 32 new signatories. In his short article on the history of *First Things First*, Poynor (1999) stated his concern that there was "a massive over-emphasis on the commercial sector of society, which consumes most of graphic designers' time, skills and creativity" (ibid, p.56). He therefore made a vital distinction between this singular, commercial role of graphic design and "the possibility […]that design might have broader purposes, potential and meanings" (ibid, p.56). Katherine McCoy, an American design educator, had earlier expressed the situation thus: "Designers must break out of the obedient, neutral, servant-to-industry mentality, an orientation that was particularly strong in the Reagan/Thatcher 1980s […] Design is not a neutral, value-free process. A design has no more integrity than its purpose or subject matter" (McCoy, 1994, p.111).

A further shift in thinking took place in 2004, when Canadian graphic designer Bruce Mau published *Massive Change – A Manifesto for the Future of Global Design.* The book and accompanying touring exhibition explored the changing forces of design in the contemporary world. Mau suggests a collaborative approach, involving other design-led disciplines focusing less on aesthetically beautiful objects, spaces, and communication, and instead more on how design can improve functionality and solve problems.

To paraphrase Marcel Duchamp, design should be liberated from the tyranny of the eye. Surveying the world, there are hundreds of examples of visionaries using design to effect positive change (Mau, 2004). This approach is supported by Jonathan Barnbrook, a radical British graphic designer and signatory of the *First Things First Manifesto 2000*:

> I realised that the critical context of graphic design isn't as simple as "get a commission, do the job for the client as best you can". It's a whole lot more complex than that […] Design shapes the environment. It helps us interact with and perceive the world. In fact, graphic design has always been a method of social change. Throughout history, leaders have facilitated social change through the distribution of printed word. It really is that simple (Design Museum, 2014).

Mau founded the Institute Without Boundaries in Toronto in collaboration with George Brown College. Here the philosophy of *massive change* was embedded in education at graduate level, fostering collaboration between disciplines to create innovative local solutions to twenty-first-century global challenges. Mau (2004) suggests the graphic designer is positioned at the centre of this approach and calls upon designers to visualise complex data and ideas before something exists as a product, service, or business. In this way, the skill of the graphic designer can allow us to see how things will look, creating a visual understanding of how things will work; this thus allows other disciplines to understand and provide service to what is initially an intangible idea.

Design can be an international language. However, design students must learn to use the power of visual language in an intercultural context, and to be the conduit for bringing together interdisciplinary communities with the ability to effect global positive change when working together.

The silos of individual design disciplines, and the students and designers who occupied them were therefore challenged. The result was the development of a "T-shaped designer" (Brown, 2009) – deep and rich in subjective knowledge, forming the vertical axis of the T, yet reaching out into new territories, disciplines, and cultures to collaborate and solve complex problems in the unchartered territory between disciplines.

Five go to Mozambique: The project

The activities of most cultures are unfathomable, unless they are viewed from within the culture, for membership of a culture provides a set of cultural eyeglasses that are the key to understanding and carrying out its activities (Brown et al., 1989, p.6).

Graphic design students from within the same year and programme began working with a German/Mozambican NGO on a live studio project to design soap packaging and publicity material for SHINE, a women's co-operative, and their supporting initiative, LIFE, a new annual film festival. In Mossuril, a coastal town in northern Mozambique, the soap co-op has been established to deliver employment for vulnerable women, and to improve the hygiene in an area where diarrhoea kills more people than HIV, AIDS, malaria, and measles combined. The town is difficult to reach by road, usually accessed by dhow from Ilha De Mozambique; infrastructure and supply chains are very limited. The design work was aligned to learning outcomes and completed within a timeframe for assessment. It was also shared online with all stakeholders in Berlin, Holland, and Mozambique, where they were able to select the most appropriate identity for the two initiatives.

The design work created a visual identity, which allowed all involved to see the soap product and the festival experience. Graphic design had given the idea form. This proved to be valuable learning for the students: graphic design was not something that was applied to existing forms and experiences; it could make them exist in the first place.

Branding is often seen and experienced by students as an activity supporting high levels of commercial or consumer activity, as challenged by the *First Things First Manifesto* of 1964 and 2000. In this case, their skills helped a small business off the ground, creating positive change in the process. They came to see that the skills they were learning on the course erased boundaries for them as designers and broadened their future workplace horizons.

The NGOs were so impressed with the selected design work that they felt some student designers could gain valuable experience by participating in their implementation in Mozambique. The NGO in Berlin proceeded to crowdfund the soap initiative, and raised nearly $6,000 for equipment.

A significant part of this success was due to the sophisticated graphics produced by the selected winner for the campaign, and the strong identity of the soap product. When the students saw their work being used to raise money globally, an interesting space of learning was created: one where current forms of entrepreneurship and graphic design skills became a powerful enabling force within an international context.

What began as an international and intercultural live studio design brief was now a proposed study of overseas community engagement with design as an enhanced student learning experience. Five students and two tutors travelled to Mozambique, and the month-long project was set as a credit-bearing module, formalising it into the assessed programme of study.

A number of cross-pollinating spaces of learning were created in this project: in the university studio, in Mozambique, in a crowdfunding campaign and in a live blog. A global landscape of interconnecting learning spaces, both real and virtual, were created for students to engage with. The designer is therefore a *connectivist*, with an inherent capacity to establish and foster links between disciplines and cultures. These skills inform how designers identify and act in situations where design can improve the wellbeing of a community, and provide solutions to economic, ecological and cultural sustainability – locally and indeed globally.

It is invaluable experience for design students to see their work implemented; in addition, this was an extraordinary opportunity to participate in international community engagement in Africa. It was hoped that the cultural learning experience in a very different environment with challenging resources and social conditions would develop student global citizenship and mobility. The NGO also saw potential for graphic design and its transformative power to change perceptions and attitudes in a country poorly served by the media.

Methodology

As previously stated, the key aim of this project was to develop student global citizenship and mobility through a cultural learning experience. Using student video interviews and evidence from reflective journals, the programme team were able to analyse the experience of implementing live design work in Mozambique. They were also able to examine the wider impact on the cohort of students and friends who did not travel to Africa but followed the experience in a live online blog.

The methodology involved recording the learning experiences of the five students using student reflective journals. Each student wrote in their journal at the end of each day, describing and evaluating their learning experience. These journals, along with photographs taken during the project, formed the content for individual books. The students were asked to review themselves and what they had recorded in their journals, and to write and design a book encompassing a reflection of their learning experience, enabling them to identify the key moments from their perspective of the process.

Reflective learning journals are widely used to reflect on encounters, moments, and experiences by briefly recording learning events that allow reflection on the meaning of the experience for an individual's own development and learning (Loo and Thorpe, 2002; Wagner, 2006). They provide up-to-date reflections on events as they happen rather than retrospectively, such as in interviews or questionnaires, and give strength to other evidence of experience.

Video interviews were recorded before, during, and after the four-week long trip to Mozambique. Extracts from the video interviews formed a documentary film, along with other footage recorded by the students and one of the tutors. One of the two tutors wrote the daily live blog, which had contributions from all of the students, charity organisers, and other volunteers. The blog page received over 3,000 visits during the four week period, and was followed by the vast majority of students on all four years of the course back home.

Intercultural communication through design

Reflective accounts alone cannot capture the effectiveness of intercultural communication as they can fail to "connect surface-level cultural norms with deeper values and cultural assumptions" (Root and Ngampornchai, 2013, p.524). Design students have the opportunity to communicate visually and creatively in their process, and through physical interaction with materials.

Observing and repeating techniques – whether with paint and brush, or keypad and computer – allows for tacit knowledge and cultural behaviour to be transferred and made explicit. The students participating in this project were able to engage in meaningful design work with local youths and so, out of necessity, had to develop communication skills and cultural awareness in order to successfully complete the design tasks in the field.

The student experience

The five students who travelled to Mozambique were selected from a pool of 12 by the Head of School, who had provided financial support to the project. The students applied for the opportunity by providing an application in the form of a motivational letter, a portfolio of research, and a CV. Four were selected: two female (students A and B) and two male (students C and D), all in their early twenties. A further male student asked to join the project, and self-financed his trip (student E).

Four students who remained at home were approached after they indicated they had been inspired by the blog, and had looked forward to reading it. Three of these students were male (students 1, 2, and 3) and one female (student 4), again in their early twenties. All students participating in the project gave written consent to the dissemination of the project and research findings.

Student pre-departure interviews

There was a shared mix of emotions prior to departure: apprehension, nervousness, and excitement. For some it felt "surreal" (A and E) to be on their way after months of anticipation and preparation. They were all looking forward to spending time in a completely different environment, to experiencing a different culture and climate, and to meeting the people of Mozambique, all of which they viewed as "a life changing experience" (C and D). In the context of their studies, they were looking forward to "re-evaluating what design could be" (A, B, and C), working with craft materials, being resourceful, and witnessing the impact of their work in action in the community (A, B, C, D, and E).

Student interviews upon return

There was a significant impact on the personal development of every student; having completed the challenge there was certainly a sense of greater self-esteem and self-confidence. They all appreciated the slower pace and relaxed attitude they found among the people of Mozambique. Despite the poverty and the health risks associated with a tropical country, the students were "humbled" (B, C, and D) by the positive and friendly attitude they found in the people of Mossuril. It made them question their priorities and attitudes associated with modern living in a developed country (C, D, and E). Student A wanted to be more "authentic […] more honest about who [she is]". Student B "learnt the art of diplomacy" and being flexible and responsive to change as it "challenged [her] thinking of preconceived ideas". The same student changed her eating habits and became more relaxed and willing to eat whatever was put in front of her: "It's matured me, I've overcome things that you don't get a chance to tackle in the UK." The experience resulted in each of them acknowledging their privilege a little more than previously.

The interviews after the students returned to the UK clearly showed that they had enjoyed a transformative experience, which they expressed in the following statements:

> For me the grass is greener than ever where I stand right now, and it's thanks to our Mozambique journey that I'm changing my way of thinking. Therefore I think it's only appropriate to say that the experience has been life changing. (A)

I am able to take more moments to pause and simply appreciate what I have. (B)

It was eye-opening to see that the locals, most of whom had so little in terms of material possessions, were in many ways happier than ourselves in the West. (C and E)

The impact on students back home

The students were interviewed five months later, just before an exhibition of the project was mounted in the University. The aim was to understand the impact of the project on the students that remained in the UK – four volunteered to be interviewed, each having followed the project by reading the live blog.

There was a keen sense of involvement from all students involved with the early live projects. They were sceptical at first – were the projects actually live? (Student 2.) Were the partners really in Mozambique? (Student 3.) Students 1, 2, and 4 commented that seeing the winning design work used in a crowdfunding campaign accompanied by the stories and films about the local community changed their opinions, and from that point forward they were all very keen to follow the progress of the project.

All the participants read the live blog several times a week for the duration of the trip, and noted in particular the large volume of writing that their fellow students had produced (3, 4). Their responses also clearly show that their understanding of graphic design changed, as they saw how it was being used:

It really made me want to have an opportunity like that, every time I read the blog I felt that a bit more. I thought it was a really good thing that you did – it just grew and grew, it was good to see how things can be made to happen, you told us – you can make anything happen, and you were right. (2)

Even if it was just for a short time when I finish University, I would like to see if I could use my skills in this way – make a difference with graphics, I didn't really consider this before now. (3)

I have been focused on getting a job in a big branding agency – I'm re-evaluating that now. (1)

Some made this point emotionally:

They all had a lot to talk about, so we felt we should read it as often as possible. I learned a lot from it, seeing the way graphics were being used – it changed my mind about graphics and what it could do completely. The day you posted the picture of the boat sail with the butterfly, I nearly started to cry. (4)

It brought tears to my eyes on occasion, I felt very proud of my peers. (1)

Conclusion

It is clear that the month the UK students spent in Mossuril has had a dramatic impact on the visibility of the NGO's work, and also on the lives of the students. It remains to be seen whether this effect will be long-term, and what legacy will have been left on the local Mossuril students. The UK students have now graduated, and we will watch to see how fearless and experimental they are in practice, after having spoken with such conviction about the inspiration they have taken from the Mossuril students. We have watched them grow as designers for four years, and know this has changed them. The philosophy embedded in the graphic design programme is now deeply embedded in them, and will resurface when they need to use it.

This project shows that design education can develop global citizenship through creative practice that engages live briefs for international charities and organisations working in the third sector. It can work by embedding students in a foreign country where they can work alongside and familiarise themselves with local people, young and old. Live projects offer an opportunity for highly motivated learning and sharing of ideas and practices with people from different cultures.

The wider impact was also positive on those students who remained in the home country. Through the sharing of the experience on the live blog, they saw the value of design in a different context: one in which it was not purely corporately driven or trivialised, but radicalised to provide economic, ecological, or cultural empowerment on a local and global stage. The project has clearly influenced them, despite their remaining at home. The experience has expanded their boundaries in terms of how they might form a meaningful career through international volunteering.

Students and teaching staff across all disciplines can begin to open their eyes to wider opportunities for social change and global citizenship through communities of interdisciplinary practice led by design and achieved through volunteering – working on real projects, where language differences have deepened the sense of individuals working in unity.

Rawsthorn (2013, p.9) argues that "design has been trivialised, misunderstood and misused" because even before the word *design* was invented, human beings had sought to change their surroundings instinctively. It was only because of the industrial age that design was redefined as a commercial tool, and is now seen as "an indulgence for spoilt consumers in developed economies, rather than as a means of helping the disadvantaged out of poverty" (ibid, p.9). The design work carried out on this project did help disadvantaged people in Mossuril. All members of the SHINE soap co-operative now have bank accounts, as the identity work carried out and implemented by the students helped create a viable business for them. The LIFE Film Festival is now in its third year, and the students who created the branding for the event continue to work on the concept with the festival organisers and local people since they graduated. The festival is a success – the students and locals have received payment for their work, and the festival continues to build capacity and provide employment.

Myrna MacLeod is a Senior Lecturer and Founding Programme Leader of the multi award-winning BDes (Hons) Graphic Design programme at Edinburgh Napier University. She teaches widely on the programme, as well as on the MA Environmental Graphic Design. Committed to using design as a force for change and good, her practice and research focuses on graphic advocacy for social justice, co-design with local and global communities, and the graphic poster culture in Scotland.

Dr Iain Macdonald is an Associate Professor and Programme Leader of MSc Creative Advertising at Edinburgh Napier University. He teaches across both the award winning Creative Advertising and BDes (Hons) and MA Graphic Design programmes drawing on his professional expertise in motion graphic design and directing commercials. His practice-led research and pedagogic research into internationalisation, the moving image and lens-based media form an argument for future directions in advertising and design practice.

References

Berman, D. (2009). *Do Good Design: How Designers Can Change The World.* Berkeley: AIGA, New Riders.

Brooks, R. and Waters, J. (2011). *Student Mobilities, Migration and the Internationalization of Higher Education.* Basingstoke: Palgrave Macmillan.

Brown, J. S., Collins, A. and Duguid, P. (1989). Situated cognition and the culture of learning. *Educational Researcher*, 18(1), 32–42.

Brown, T. (2009). *Change by Design: How Design Thinking Transforms Organizations and Inspires Innovation.* New York: Harper Business.

Design Museum (2014). *Barnbrook: Pioneering the Notion of Graphic Design with a Social Conscience* [Online]. Available at: http://designmuseum.org/designers/jonathan-barnbrook [Accessed 22 April 2016].

Garland, K. (1964). *First Things First Manifesto.* London: Privately Published [Online]. Available at: http://www.designishistory.com/1960/first-things-first/ [Accessed 22 April 2016].

Loo, R. and Thorpe, K. (2002). Using reflective learning journals to improve individual and team performance. *Team Performance Management*, 8 (5), 134–139.

Mau, B. (2004). *Massive Change: A Manifesto for the Future of Global Design: A Manifesto for the Future Design Culture*. London: Phaidon.

McCoy, K. (1994). Countering the tradition of the apolitical designer. In Myerson, J. (Ed.). *Design Renaissance: Selected Papers from the International Design Congress, Glasgow, Scotland 1993*. Horsham: Open Eye, 105–114.

Mendoza, H. R. and Matyók, T. (2013). Designing Student Citizenship: Internationalised Education in Transformative Disciplines. *International Journal of Art & Design Education*, 32(2), 215–225.

Poynor, R. (1999). First things first: A brief history. *Adbusters*, 27, 54–56.

Rawsthorn, A. (2013). *Hello World: Where Design Meets Life*. London: Penguin.

Root, E. and Ngampornchai, A. (2013). "I came back as a new human being": student descriptions of intercultural competence acquired through education abroad experiences. *Journal of Studies in International Education,* 17 (5), 515–532.

Wagner, Z. M. (2006). Using student journals for course evaluation. *Assessment and Evaluation in Higher Education*, 24(3), 261–272.

Waters, J., Brooks, R. and Pimlott-Wilson, H. (2011). Youthful escapes? British students, overseas education and the pursuit of happiness. *Social and Cultural Geography*, 12 (5), 455–469.